A-Z CHESTE

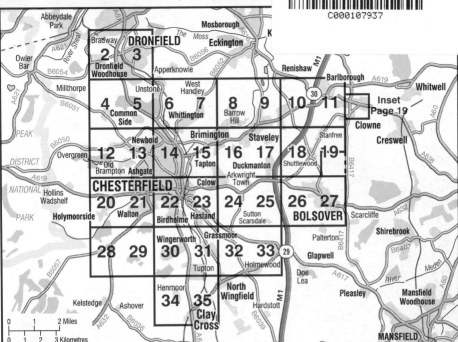

Reference

Motorway	**M1**	
A Road	**A61**	
B Road	**B6051**	
Dual Carriageway		
One-way Street Traffic flow on A roads is indicated by a heavy line on the driver's left.	→	
Restricted Access		
Pedestrianized Road		
Track		
Footpath		
Residential Walkway		
Railway	Tunnel / Station Level Crossing	

Built-up Area	*DUKE ST.*	
Local Authority Boundary		
Postcode Boundary		
Map Continuation	**23**	
Car Park (selected)	**P**	
Church or Chapel	†	
Fire Station	■	
Hospital	**H**	
House Numbers (A & B Roads only)	27 / 8	
Information Centre	**i**	
National Grid Reference	370	

Police Station	▲
Post Office	★
Toilet	▽
with facilities for the Disabled	♿
Educational Establishment	⌐
Hospital or Hospice	⌐
Industrial Building	⌐
Leisure or Recreational Facility	⌐
Place of Interest	⌐
Public Building	⌐
Shopping Centre or Market	⌐
Other Selected Buildings	⌐

Scale 1:15,840

4 inches (10.16 cm) to 1 mile
6.31cm to 1kilometre

0 — ¼ — ½ Mile
0 — 250 — 500 — 750 Metres — 1 Kilometre

Copyright of Geographers' A-Z Map Company Ltd.

Head Office :
Fairfield Road, Borough Green, Sevenoaks, Kent TN15 8PP
Tel: 01732 781000 (Enquiries & Trade Sales)
01732 783422 (Retail Sales)
www.a-zmaps.co.uk
Copyright © Geographers' A-Z Map Co. Ltd. 2004

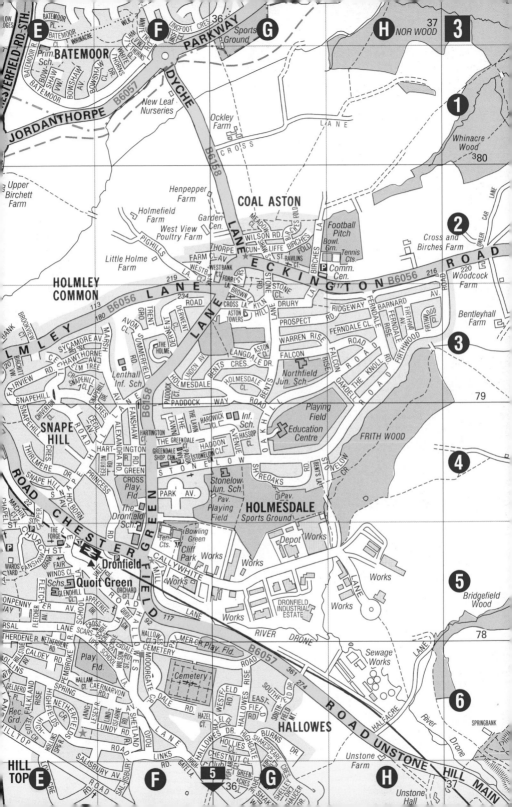

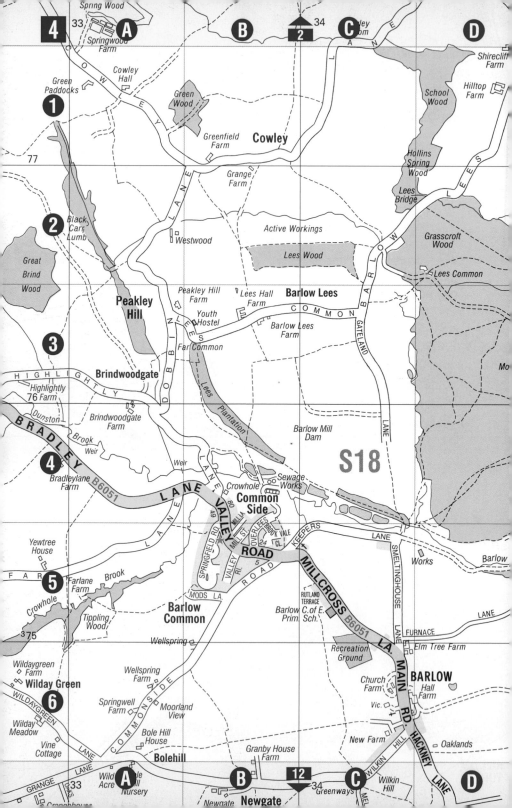

Little Foxstone Wood

Foxstone Dam

Old Furnace Wood

1 Nether Handley

NORTH EAST DERBYSHIRE
CHESTERFIELD

Belle Vue Farm

Eyries Farm

2

White Lodge

Hagge Farm

Hopewell Wood

3

Breck Farm

S43

76 **7**

Monument

Breck Farm Cottages

Foxlowe Junction

Claypit

HILL GROVE ROAD

BROOKS ROAD

4

BARROW HILL

Recreation Ground

WHITTINGTON

Sports Pav Ground

Pavilion

Rec Grd

SOUTHGATE WOODFORD CHELMSFORD WAY

MIDLAND WAY

TRAFFIC TER

ALLPORT

DRIVE

Playground

CAMPBELL

Barrow Hill Museum

ROAD

STATION

CHIGWELL WAY ROMFORD WAY WESTLANDS

DUEWELL CT.

Barrow Hill Primary Sch.

5 Heywood Farm

RIVER ROTHER

3·75

CAVENDISH PL.

WORKS

Rec. Grd.

Summit Sidings

Works

Works

Nature Trail

Factory

Chemical Works

6 Way

Victoria Farm

Hounsfield Bridge

Sports Grd.

Club

ROAD

HOLLINGWOOD

RIVER

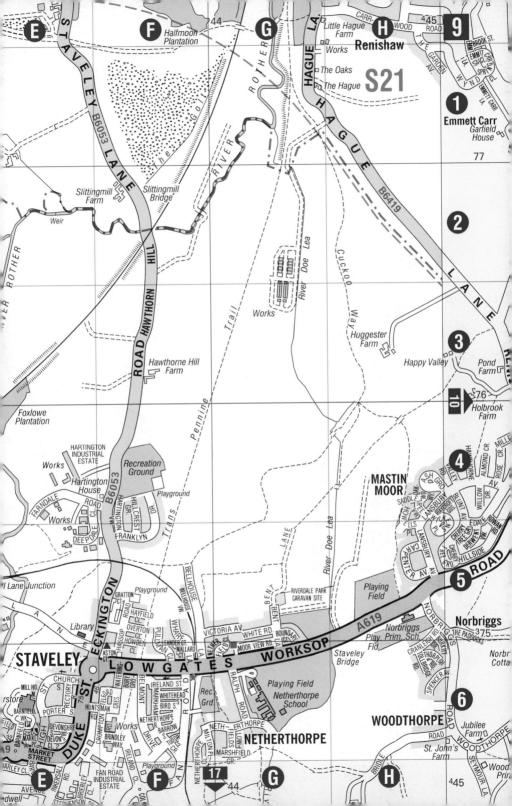

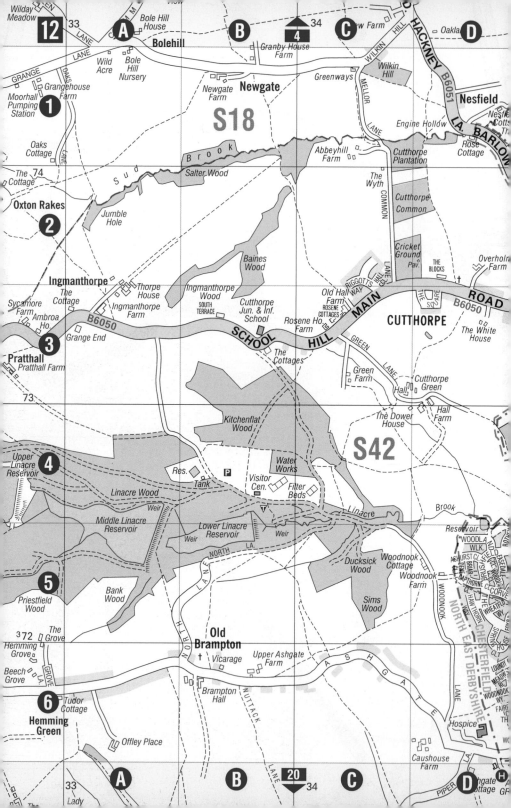

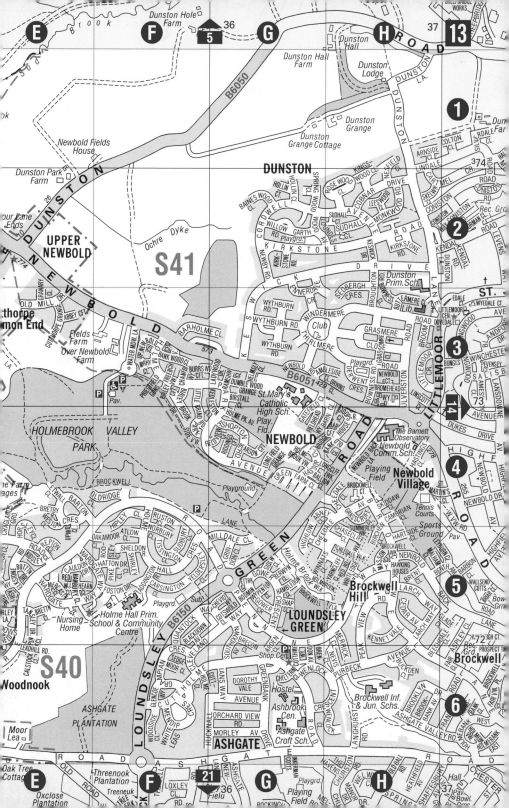

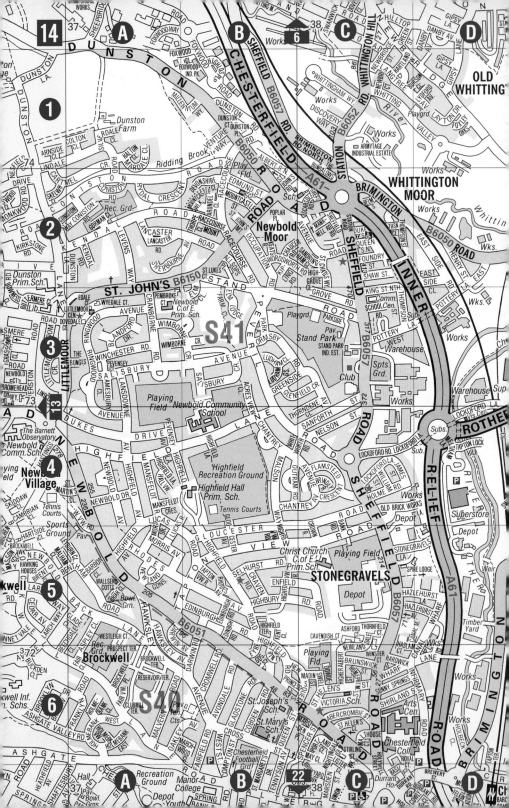

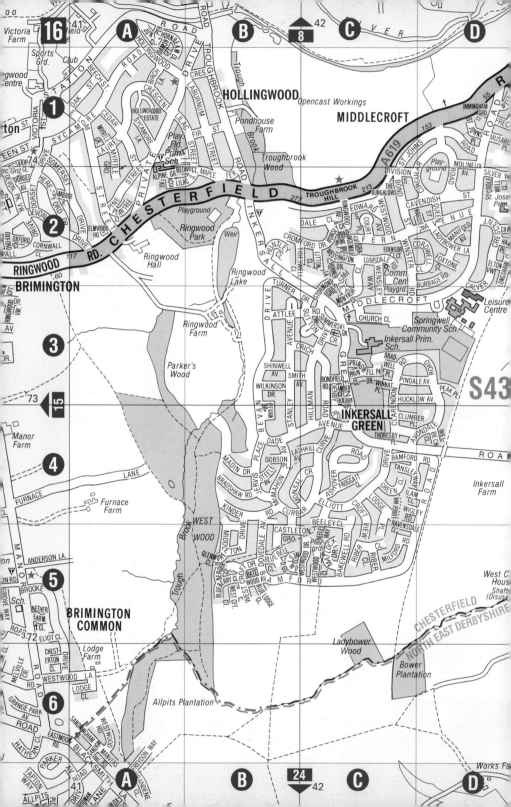

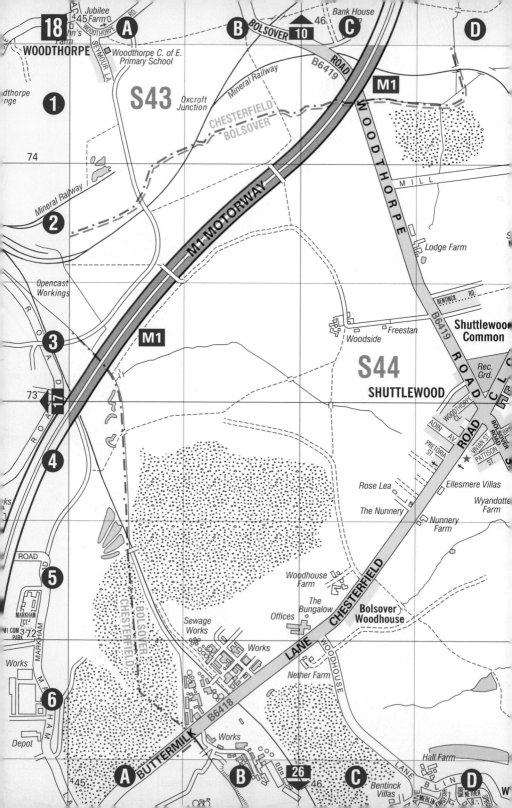

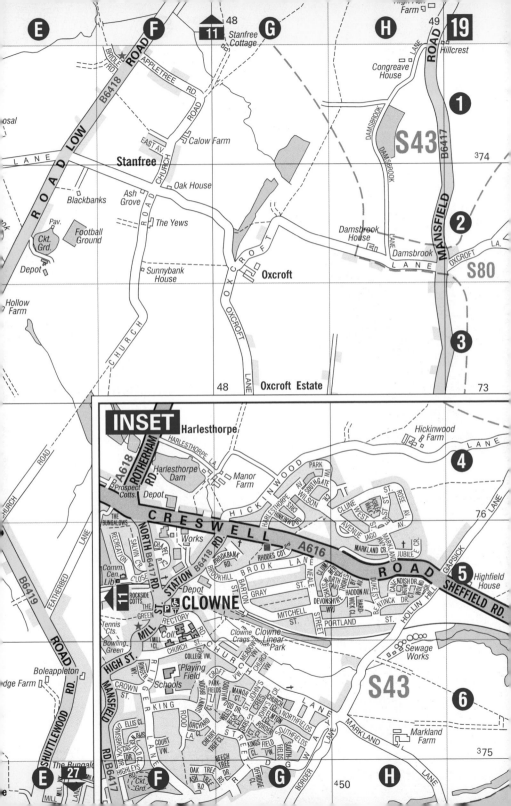

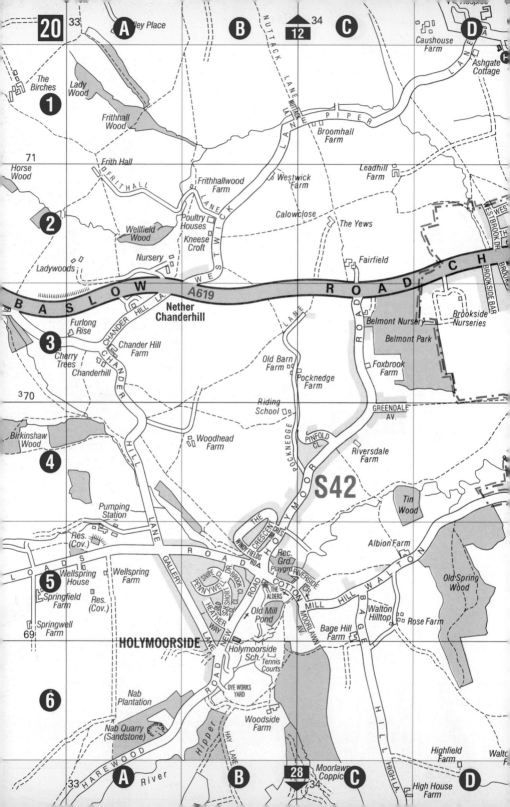

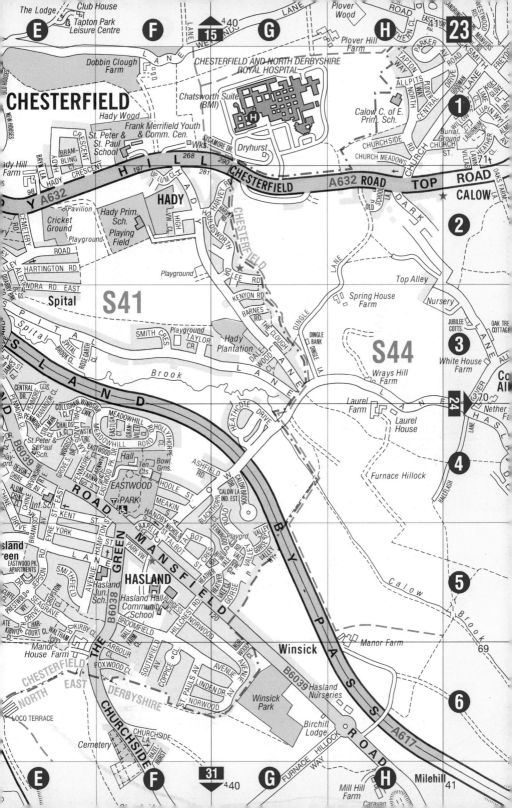

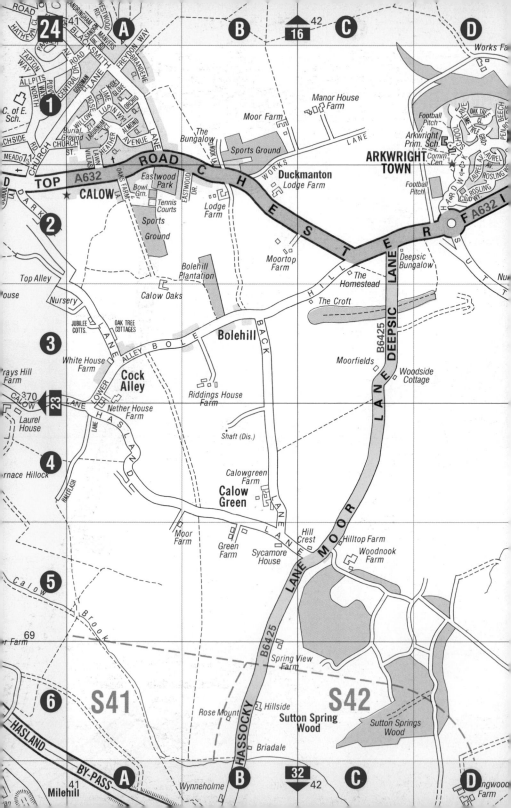

The Bungalow Works Sutherland Farm
SHUTTLE-WOOD RD. MILL LANE Cemetery
MILL WK. Long Acre
MILL LANE Wyndcroft
Rec. Grd. **Limekiln Field**
TOP B6419 ROAD QUARRY RD.
WINMILL FIELDS BANK CL.
NEW S. LIMEKILN
HILL TOP B6419 ROAD BARTON CL.
STRATTON CL. SIDES GN.
DYKES GARDENERS CL.
OXCROFT The Orchard Bungalow
LONGLANDS STEEL LANE
1 WHALEY RD.
Keepers Hollow LANE
Nook Villa
Farnsworth Farm
Pond House Highfield House
71
BOLSOVER MOOR

HILL ROAD
Council Offs. PEGASUS CT.
CASTLE ST. TOWN END
CHURCH TOWN END
HIGH ST. MK PL.
STREET Hall
of E. ool HORSECROFT ROAD

WELBECK ROAD MARLPIT LANE
ELMTON LANE
Strathyre Ty-Gwyn **H** BOLSOVER HOSPITAL
Sycamore House
MEADOWLANDS
BECK CL. CEDAR PK. DR.
TSWTH CL.
HORSEHEAD BRETTON AV.
CORNMILL SYCAMORE CL.
Bolsover Inf. Sch. Play. Fld.
Playing Field Pav.
RIDGEWAY HOLY BECK
TREE CL. CHERRY ROAD
SANDHILLS ARUNUM CL. LILAC STABLES CT.
ELM CL. HORSEHEAD LA.
Pondfield Bungalow
2 B6417
Glenavon Greenacres
LANGSTONE AV. MOORACRE LANE
3 370

Hall Pav.
SMITHSON AV.
PORTLAND MOORFIELD SQ.
PORTLAND CR. HUNTLY MOORFIELD AV.
MOORFIELD SOUTH CAVENDISH
MORVEN AVENUE SCHOOL FIELD CR. ST. LAWRENCE
TOWER CR. CLAY CL.
CROWN SCHOOL FIELD CL.
CONDUIT STATION ROAD
LANGWITH ROAD
Bolsover School (Moorfield Hall)
Bolsover Moor Farm
Tennis Courts Playing Field
LANGWITH ROAD
4

STATION ROAD LORDS CL.
HIGHFIELD RD. SEARSON AV.
BROOKFIELD RD. SPITTAL GREEN
AVONDALE RD. FAIRFIELD RD.
MEADOW DR. EASTERN AV.
OWLCOTES STOCKLEY VW.
DARWOOD CRICH VW.
HUDSON MOUNT VICTORIA ST. CROSS ST.
MIDDLE ST. **A632** WELLS ST. ROAD
NESBITT ST. SELWYN ST. STREET
SUTTON VIEW **Hillstown**
WEST VIEW
The Meadows Hawthorns
CASTLE GREEN Playing Field
VALLEY VW. PLEASANT AV. EAST VW.

ROTHERHAM B6417

ROAD
69

5

BUDGET LA.
6 MAIN ST.
MANSFIELD RD. EAST ST.

Palterton
CASTLE VIEW THIRTEEN ROW STEEL'S LANE
PENNINE TER. BACK
MAIN ST. Playing Field
MANSFIELD ROAD NORTHFIELD LANE
LANE **Scarcliffe**

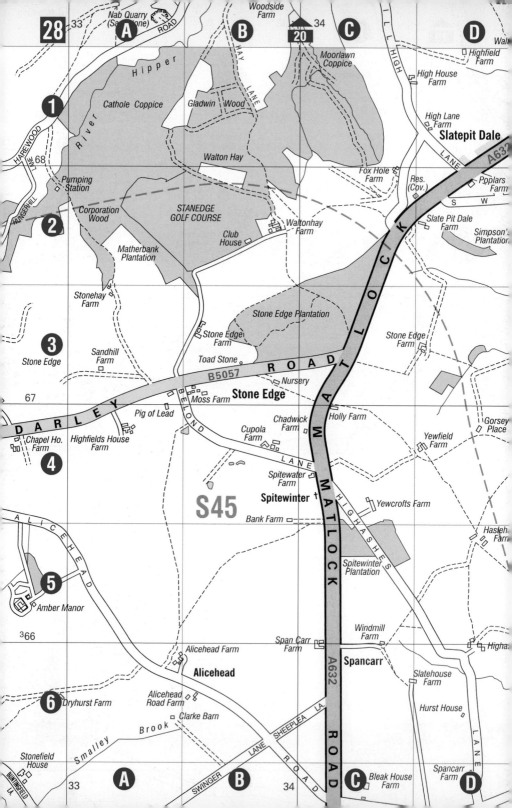

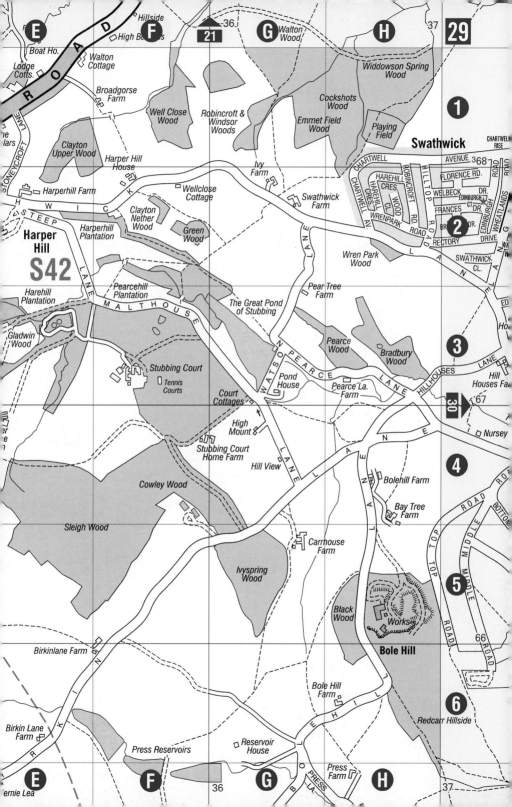

E

Hillside
High Be... s
F

36
21

G Walton Wood

H

37

Boat Ho.
Walton Cottage
Lodge Cotts.
Broadgorse Farm
Well Close Wood
Robincroft & Windsor Woods
Widdowson Spring Wood
Cockshots Wood
Emmet Field Wood
Playing Field

Clayton Upper Wood
Harper Hill House
Ivy Farm
Swathwick
CHARTWELL RISE

1

Harperhill Farm
Wellclose Cottage
Swathwick Farm
CHARTWELL AVENUE 368
HAREHILL CRES.
ROBINCROFT WOOD
FLORENCE RD.
WELBECK DR.
EDINBURGH CT.
FRANCES DR.
WHEATLANDS
CHARTWELL AV.
HAREHILL CRES.
CHARTWELL CRES.
WREN PARK
RECTORY DRIVE
EDINBURGH DR.

STONECROFT LANE

H W I C K
STEEP
Clayton Nether Wood
Green Wood
Wren Park Wood
SWATHWICK CL.

2

Harper Hill
S42
Harperhill Plantation
Pearcehill Plantation
The Great Pond of Stubbing
Pear Tree Farm

ED

Ho

Harehill Plantation
M A L T H O U S E
Pearce Wood
Bradbury Wood

3

HILLHOUSES
LANE
Hill Houses Fa

Gladwin Wood
Stubbing Court
Tennis Courts
Pond House
Pearce La. Farm
Pearce La.

W A T S O N
P E A R C E L A N E

30
67

Court Cottages
High Mount
Stubbing Court Home Farm
Hill View
Nursey

L A N E

N

Bolehill Farm

4

Cowley Wood
Bay Tree Farm

ROAD

TOP ROAD

Sleigh Wood
Carrhouse Farm

L A N E

BOTTOM

Birkinlane Farm
Ivyspring Wood
Black Wood
Works

MIDDLE ROAD

5

66

Bole Hill

Birkin Lane Farm
K I R K I N
Bole Hill Farm

6

Redcarr Hillside

E

F

G

H

36

Reservoir House
Press Farm
37

Press Reservoirs

P R E S S L A.

ernie Lea

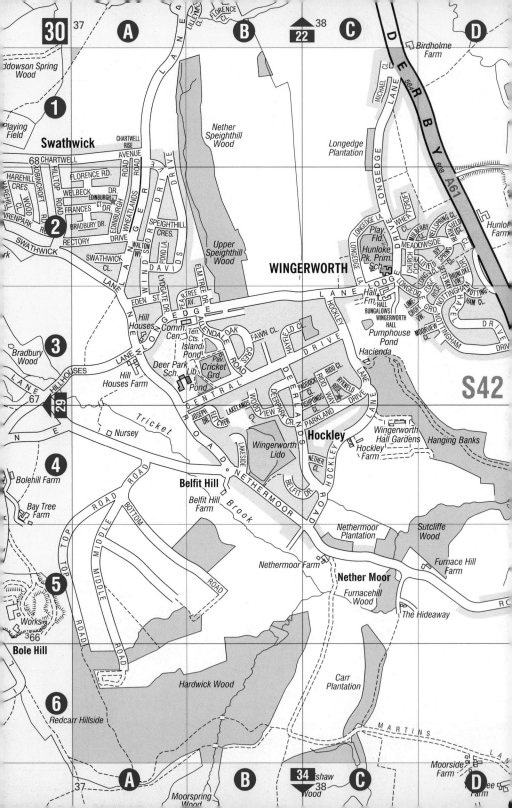

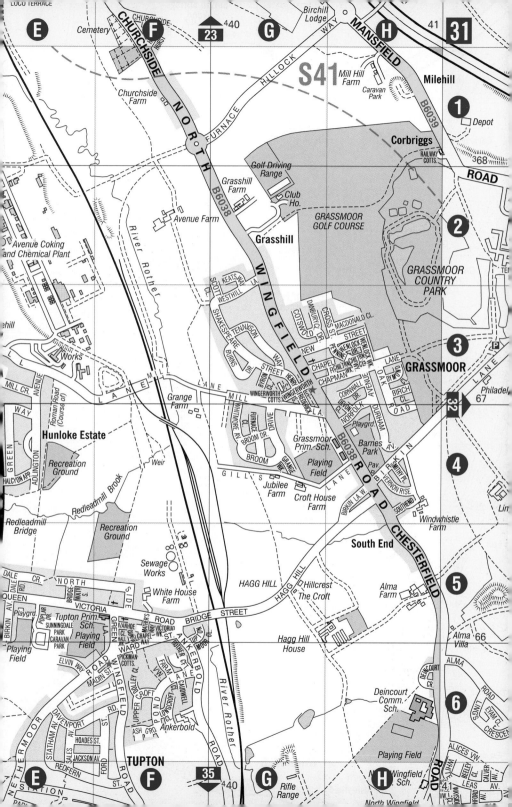

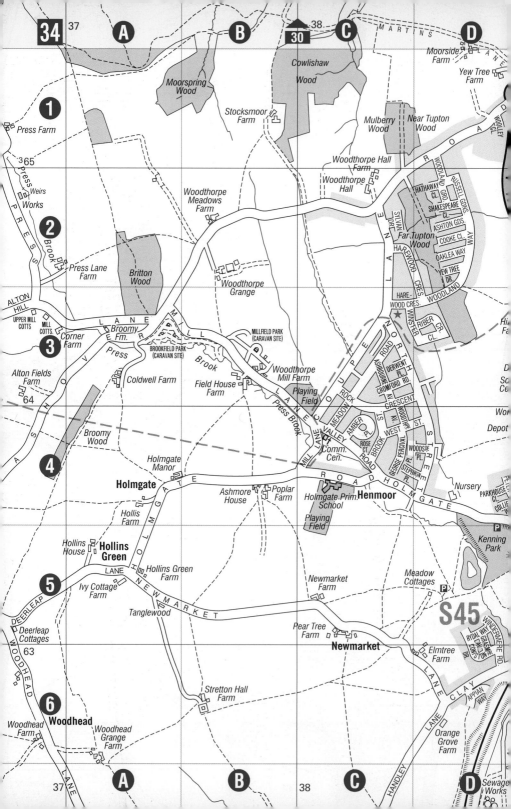

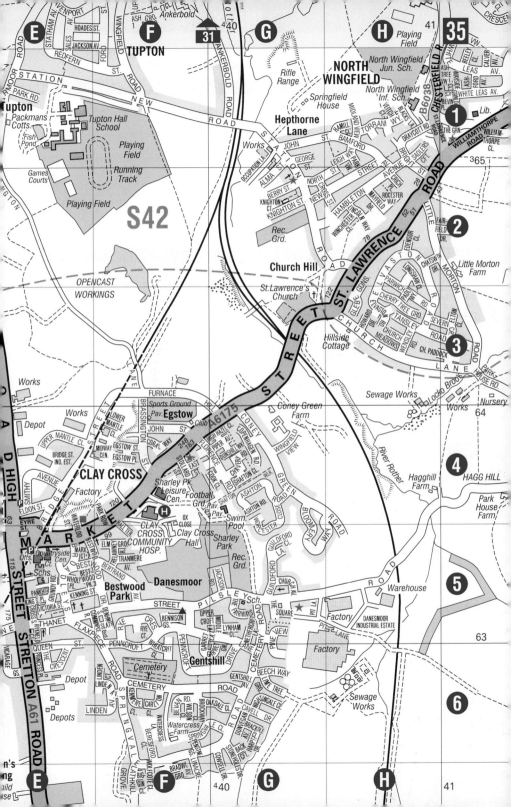

INDEX

Including Streets, Places & Areas, Hospitals & Hospices, Industrial Estates,
Selected Flats & Walkways and Selected Places of Interest.

HOW TO USE THIS INDEX

1. Each street name is followed by its Posttown or Postal Locality and then by its map reference; e.g. Abbey Cft. *Ches* . . . .3E **13** is in the Chesterfield Posttown and is to be found in square 3E on page **13**. The page number being shown in bold type.
A strict alphabetical order is followed in which Av., Rd., St., etc. (though abbreviated) are read in full and as part of the street name; e.g. Ashurst Clo. appears after Ash Tree Vw. but before Ash Va.

2. Streets and a selection of Subsidiary names not shown on the Maps, appear in the index in *Italics* with the thoroughfare to which it is connected shown in brackets; e.g. *Appletree Wlk. Dron* . . . .*5F* **3** *(off Appletree Dri.)*

3. Places and areas are shown in the index in **blue type**, the map reference to the actual map square in which the Town or Area is located and not to the place name; e.g. **Arkwright Town**. . . . **1D 24**

4. An example of a selected place of interest is **Barrow Hill Mus.** **5A 8**

5. An example of a hospital or hospice is **ASHGATE HOSPICE.** . . . **6D 12**

GENERAL ABBREVIATIONS

All : Alley	Ct : Court	Lit : Little	Rd : Road
App : Approach	Cres : Crescent	Lwr : Lower	Shop : Shopping
Arc : Arcade	Cft : Croft	Mc : Mac	S : South
Av : Avenue	Dri : Drive	Mnr : Manor	Sq : Square
Bk : Back	E : East	Mans : Mansions	Sta : Station
Boulevd : Boulevard	Embkmt : Embankment	Mkt : Market	St : Street
Bri : Bridge	Est : Estate	Mdw : Meadow	Ter : Terrace
B'way : Broadway	Fld : Field	M : Mews	Trad : Trading
Bldgs : Buildings	Gdns : Gardens	Mt : Mount	Up : Upper
Bus : Business	Gth : Garth	Mus : Museum	Va : Vale
Cvn : Caravan	Ga : Gate	N : North	Vw : View
Cen : Centre	Gt : Great	Pal : Palace	Vs : Villas
Chu : Church	Grn : Green	Pde : Parade	Vis : Visitors
Chyd : Churchyard	Gro : Grove	Pk : Park	Wlk : Walk
Circ : Circle	Ho : House	Pas : Passage	W : West
Cir : Circus	Ind : Industrial	Pl : Place	Yd : Yard
Clo : Close	Info : Information	Quad : Quadrant	
Comn : Common	Junct : Junction	Res : Residential	
Cotts : Cottages	La : Lane	Ri : Rise	

POSTTOWN AND POSTAL LOCALITY ABBREVIATIONS

Alt : Alton	*Cor* : Corbriggs	*Ink* : Inkersall	*Scar* : Scarcliffe
App : Apperknowle	*Cut* : Cutthorpe	*Kil* : Killamarsh	*Shef* : Sheffield
Ark T : Arkwright Town	*Dane* : Danesmoor	*Lwr P* : Lower Pilsley	*Shut* : Shuttlewood
Ash : Ashgate	*Dron* : Dronfield	*Mar L* : Marsh Lane	*Stanf* : Stanfree
Asvr : Ashover	*Dron W* : Dronfield Woodhouse	*Mas M* : Mastin Moor	*Stav* : Staveley
Blbgh : Barlborough	*Duck* : Duckmanton	*Mid H* : Middle Handley	*Sut S* : Sutton Scarsdale
Barl : Barlow	*E'mr* : Eastmoor	*New T* : New Tupton	*Temp N* : Temple Normanton
Bar H : Barrow Hill	*Eck* : Eckington	*New W* : New Whittington	*Tup* : Tupton
Bsvr : Bolsover	*Gras* : Grassmoor	*N Wing* : North Wingfield	*Uns* : Unstone
Brim : Brimington	*Has* : Hasland	*Old Br* : Old Brampton	*Walt* : Walton
Cal : Calow	*Heath* : Heath	*Old T* : Old Tupton	*Wing* : Wingerworth
Ches : Chesterfield	*Holl* : Hollingwood	*Old W* : Old Whittington	*Whit M* : Whittington Moor
Clay C : Clay Cross	*Holm* : Holmesfield	*Pal* : Palterton	*Wing* : Wingerworth
Clow : Clowne	*Hlmwd* : Holmewood	*Pool* : Poolsbrook	
Coal A : Coal Aston	*Holy* : Holymoorside	*Ren* : Renishaw	

A

	Alders, The. *Holy* 5B **20**	Alma Rd. *N Wing* 6A **32**	Ambleside Dri. *Bsvr* 3D **26**
	Alexandra Rd. *Dron* 4F **3**	Alma St. *N Wing* 2G **35**	Amesbury Clo. *Ches* 3A **14**
	Alexandra Rd. E. *Ches* 2E **23**	Alma St. W. *Ches*. 2A **22**	Anderson Clo.
Abbey Cft. *Ches*. 3E **13**	Alexandra Rd. W. *Ches* . . .1B **22**	Almond Clo. *Cal*. 1A **24**	New W 5G **7**
Abbeyhill Clo. *Ash* 6D **12**	Alford Clo. *Ches* 1G **21**	Almond Cres.	Anderson La. *Brim* 5H **15**
Abercrombie St. *Ches* 6C **14**	Alicehead. 6B **28**	*Mas M* 4A **10**	Angel Yd. *Ches* 1C **22**
Abney Clo. *Ches* 4G **13**	Alicehead Rd. *Asvr* 4A **28**	Almond Pl. *Brim* 3G **15**	Anglesey Rd. *Dron*. 6E **3**
Acacia Av. *Holl*. 2A **16**	Alices Vw. *N Wing* 6A **32**	Alpine Gro. *Holl* 2A **16**	Ankerbold Rd. *Old T*. 6F **31**
Acorn Ridge. *Walt* 5F **21**	Alice Way. *Uns*. 3A **6**	Alport Ri. *Dron W* 4B **2**	Annesley Clo. *Has* 4E **23**
Acres Vw. Clo. *Ches*. 3B **14**	Allendale Rd. *Wing* 3B **30**	Alton Clo. *Dron W* 6B **2**	Appian Way. *Clay C*. 6D **34**
Adelphi Way. *Stav* 2E **17**	Allestree Dri. *Dron W*. 5A **2**	Alton Clo. *Walt*. 4F **21**	Appletree Dri. *Dron* 5E **3**
Adin Av. *Shut*. 4D **18**	Allpits Rd. *Cal* 1H **23**	Alton Hill. *Alt* 3A **34**	Appletree Rd. *Stanf* 1F **19**
Adlington Av. *Wing* 4E **31**	Allport Ter. *Bar H* 4B **8**	Alum Chine Clo. *Has* 4E **23**	Appletree Wlk. *Dron*. 5F **3**
Albert Av. *New W*. 5F **7**	Allsops Pl. *Ches*. 2B **14**	Amber Cres. *Ches* 3G **21**	*(off Appletree Dri.)*
Albert Rd. *New W* 5F **7**	Alma Cres. *Dron* 3E **3**	Amber Cft. *Ink*. 3C **16**	Arbour Clo. *Ches* 6F **23**
Albert St. N. *Ches* 1B **14**	Alma Leisure Pk.	Amber Pl. *Clay C* 4C **34**	Arden Clo. *Ches*. 6G **13**
Albion Rd. *Ches*. 1B **22**	*Ches*. 3D **22**	Ambleside Clo. *Ches* 3G **13**	Ardsley Rd. *Ches* 1F **21**

Arklow Clo. *Has* 4D 22
Arkwright Town. 1D 24
Armytage Ind. Est.
   Whit M 2D 14
   (Brimington Rd. N.)
Armytage Ind. Est.
   Whit M 1C 14
   (Station Rd.)
Arnside Clo. *Ches* 1H 13
Arundel Clo. *Ches* 2B 14
Arundel Clo. *Dron W* 5B 2
Arundel Ct. *Stav* *6E 9*
   (off Devonshire St.)
Ashbourne Av. *Clay C* . . . 3C 34
Ashbourne Clo. *Ches* 5E 13
Ashcroft Dri. *Old W* 5D 6
Ashdown Dri. *Ches* 3H 21
Ashfield Rd. *Has* 4F 23
Ashford Av.
   N Wing. . . . 1H 35 & 6A 32
Ashford Clo. *Dron W* 6B 2
Ashford Ct. *Ches* 5C 14
Ashford Rd. *Dron W* 6B 2
Ashgate. **6G 13**
Ashgate Av. *Ches* 1G 21
ASHGATE HOSPICE. 6D 12
Ashgate Rd. *Ash* 6C 12
Ashgate Rd. *Ches* 6F 13
Ashgate Valley Rd.
   Ches 6H 13
ASH GREEN. 1D 20
Ash Gro. *Mas M* 4H 9
Ash Gro. *Tup* 6F 31
Ashlea Wlk. *Clow*. 4H 19
Ashleigh Clo. *Old W* 5D 6
Ashleigh Rd. *Blbgh* 1F 11
Ashopton Rd. *Ches* 4G 13
Ashover Rd.
   Clay C & Old T 4A 34
Ashover Rd. *Ink* 4C 16
Ashton Clo. *Ches* 4G 13
Ashton Gdns. *Old T* 2D 34
Ash Tree Clo. *Ches* 1G 21
Ash Tree Rd. *Clow* 6F 19
Ash Tree Vw.
   N Wing. . . . . 6A 32 & 1H 35
Ashurst Clo. *Ches* 5D 12
Aspley Clo. *Ches* 6A 14
Aston Clo. *Dron*. 3G 3
Aston Ct. *Stav* 6F 9
Aston Towers. *Dron*. 3G 3
Astwith Clo. *Hlmwd*. 5F 33
Atholl Clo. *Walt* 4F 21
Atkinson Ct. *Ches*. 3C 22
Atlantic Cres. *Shef*. 1C 2
Atlantic Rd. *Shef* 1B 2
Atlow Clo. *Ches* 5F 13
Attlee Rd. *Ink*. 3B 16
Auckland's Pl. *Ches* 2C 22
Avenue 1. *Has* 4D 22
Avenue 2. *Has*. 4D 22
Avenue 3. *Has*. 4D 22
Avenue 4. *Has*. 4D 22
Avenue 5. *Has*. 4D 22
Avenue 6. *Has*. 4D 22
Avenue 7. *Has*. 4D 22
Avenue 8. *Has*. 4D 22
Avenue Rd. *Ches* 2C 14
Avenue, The. *Dron* 4F 3
Aviemore Clo.
   New W. 4G 7
Avon Clo. *Dron*. 3F 3
Avondale Rd. *Bsvr*. 4E 27
Avondale Rd. *Ches*. 6B 14
Avondale Rd. *Ink*. 4D 16

B

Back Cft. *Dane*. 6G 35
Back La. *Cal*. 3B 24

Back La. *Pal* 6F 27
Bk. South St. *New W* 5F 7
   (in two parts)
Bacons La. *Ches* 4B 22
Bacon's Spring. 6D 34
Baden Powell Av.
   Ches. 3B 22
Baden Powell Rd.
   Ches 2C 22
Badger Clo. *Walt* 4F 21
Bage Hill. *Walt*. 5C 20
Bainbridge Rd. *Bsvr* 3D 26
Baines Wood Clo.
   Ches. 2G 13
Bakewell Rd. *Ink* 5C 16
Ballidon Clo. *Ches*. 4G 13
Balmoak La. *Ches*. 4E 15
Balmoral Cres. *Dron W* . . 4B 2
Balmoral Way. *New W* . . . 4G 7
Bamford Av. *N Wing* 1H 35
Bamford Rd. *Ink*. 5B 16
Bamford St. *New W* 4F 7
Bank Clo. *Bsvr*. 1E 27
Bank Ct. *Brim*. 2F 15
Bank Rd. *Ches*. 4C 14
Bank St. *Brim*. 2F 15
Bank St. *Ches* 1A 22
Bank Wood Clo. *Ches*. . . . 3F 13
Barbon Clo. *Ches*. 5A 14
Barclay Grange. *Ches*. . . . 1D 22
Bar Cft. *Ches*. 4H 13
Barholme Clo. *Ches*. 3F 13
Barker Fold. *Ches*. 1H 21
Barker La. *Ches*. 1H 21
Barlborough. 1E 11
Barlborough Common.
   . . . . **3F 11**
Barlborough Low Common.
   . . . . **1B 10**
Barlborough Rd.
   Clow. 3H 11
Barley La. *Ash*. 5E 13
Barley M. *Dron W*. 4A 2
Barlow. **6C 4**
Barlow Common. **5B 4**
Barlow Lees. **3B 4**
Barlow Lees La. *Dron*. 3C 4
Barlow Rd. *Ches*. 1D 12
Barlow Rd. *Stav*. 1E 17
Barlow Vw. *Dron*. 1F 5
Barnard Av. *Coal A*. 3H 3
Barn Clo. *Ches*. 4H 13
Barnes Av. *Dron W* 4B 2
Barnes La. *Dron W* 2A 2
   (in two parts)
Barnes Rd. *Ches*. 3G 23
Barnfield Clo. *Hlmwd*. . . . 6E 33
Barnfield Rd. *Stav*. 6E 9
Barnfield Ter. *Stav*. 6E 9
Barnfield Wlk. *Stav*. 6E 9
Barnham Clo. *Ches*. 4F 21
Barrow Hill. **4B 8**
Barrow Hill Mus.. . . . . 5A 8
Barrow St. *Stav*. 6F 9
Barry Rd. *Brim*. 6H 15
Barton Cres. *Ches*. 4E 13
Barton St. *Clow*. 5G 19
Basil Clo. *Ches*. 1C 22
Baslow Rd. *E'mr*. 3A 20
Bateman Clo. *New W*. 4F 7
Batemoor. **1E 3**
Batemoor Clo. *Shef*. 1E 3
Batemoor Pl. *Shef*. 1E 3
Batemoor Rd. *Shef*. 1E 3
Batemoor Wlk. *Shef*. *1E 3*
   (off Batemoor Clo.)
Batewood Av. *Ink*. 5B 16
Bathurst Rd. *Bsvr*. 4C 26
Baycliff Dri. *Ches*. 1G 21
Beck Clo. *Bsvr*. 2G 27
Becket Av. *Shef*. 1B 2
Becket Cres. *Shef*. 1C 2
Becket Wlk. *Shef*. 1B 2

Beechdale Clo. *Ches* 6H 13
Beech Dri. *Ark T* 1D 24
Beech Gro. *Duck*. 6G 17
Beech St. *Holl* 1A 16
Beech Tree Dri. *Clow*. . . . 6G 19
Beech Way. *Dane*. 6G 35
Beech Way. *Dron* 3E 3
Beechwood Rd. *Dron* 5D 2
Beehive Rd. *Ches* 2H 21
Beehive Yd. *Ches*. 2H 21
Beeley Clo. *Ink* 4C 16
Beeley Clo.
   N Wing. . . . . 6A 32 & 1H 35
Beeley Vw. *Walt*. 5G 21
Beeley Way. *Ink*. 5C 16
Beeston Clo. *Dron W* 4A 2
Beetwell St. *Ches*. 2C 22
Belfit Dri. *Wing*. 4B 30
Belfit Hill. **4B 30**
Belle Vue Clo. *Brim* 2F 15
Bellhouse La. *Stav*. 5F 9
Bellhouse Vw. *Stav*. 5F 9
Belmont Dri. *Stav*. 6F 9
Belmont St. *Ches*. 2C 14
Belond La. *Asvr*. 4B 28
Belton Clo. *Dron W* 5A 2
Belvedere Av. *Ches* 4A 22
Belvedere Clo. *Ches*. 4E 21
Bennimoor Way.
   Ches. 4A 22
Bennison Gdns. *Dane*. . . . 5F 35
Bentham Rd. *Ches* 5A 14
Bentinck Dri. *Clow*. 5H 19
Bentinck Rd. *Shut*. 3D 18
Bentinck Vs. *Bsvr*. 1C 26
Bent La. *Stav*. 5G 9
Bents Cres. *Dron*. 3G 3
Bents La. *Dron*. 3G 3
   (in two parts)
Beresford Clo. *Dane*. 6F 35
Bernard Clo. *Brim*. 2H 15
Berry St. *N Wing*. 2G 35
Bertrand Av. *Clay C*. 5F 35
Berwick Av. *Ches*. 5G 21
Berwick Clo. *Ches*. 5G 21
Berwick Ct. *Ches*. 5G 21
Berwyn Clo. *Ches*. 5G 13
Bestwood Dri. *Clay C*. . . . 5E 35
   (in two parts)
Bestwood Park. **5F 35**
Bestwood Pk. *Clay C*. . . . 5E 35
Bevan Dri. *Ink*. 4B 16
Bevan Rd. *Dane*. 6F 35
Bevin Pl. *N Wing*. 1H 35
Biggin Clo. *Dane*. 6F 35
Bilby La. *Brim*. 1G 15
Birch Clo. *Gras*. 3H 31
Birchen Clo. *Ches*. 5H 13
Birchen Clo. *Dron W*. 5B 2
Birches Fold. *Coal A*. 2G 3
Birches La. *Coal A*. 2G 3
Birch Hall Golf Course.
   . . . . 3A 6
Birch Holt Gro. *Uns*. 3A 6
Birchitt Clo. *Shef*. 1A 2
Birchitt Pl. *Shef*. 1A 2
Birchitt Rd. *Shef*. 1A 2
Birchitt Vw. *Dron*. 3E 3
Birch Kiln Cft. *Brim*. 3H 15
Birch La. *Holl*. 1A 16
Birchwood Ct. *Ches*. 5B 22
Birchwood Cres.
   Ches. 5B 22
Birdholme. **5C 22**
Birdholme Cres. *Ches*. . . . 4C 22
Bird St. *Stav*. 6F 9
Birkdale Dri. *Ches*. 5H 21
Birkin Av. *New T*. 5E 31
Birkin La. *Asvr*. 6E 29
Birkin La. *Gras*. 4H 31
Birkin La. W. *Gras*. 4H 31
Birley Brook Dri. *Ches*. . . . 3F 13

Birley Cft. *Ches* 3F 13
Birstall Clo. *Ches*. 3G 13
Bishops Wlk. *Ches*. 4C 22
Bishops Way *Ches*. 4C 22
Blackdown Av. *Ches*. 5F 13
Blacks La. *N Wing*. 1H 35
Blacksmith La. *Cal*. 6A 16
Blackthorn Clo. *Has*. 4F 23
Blandford Dri. *Ches*. 3A 14
Blind La. *Bsvr*. 1D 26
Blocks, The. *Cut*. 2D 12
Bloomery Way *Clay C*. . . . 4G 35
Bluebank Vw. *New W*. 5F 7
Bluebell Clo. *Blbgh*. 2F 11
Bluebell Clo. *Ink*. 5B 16
Blueberry Clo. *Ink*. 5B 16
Bluelodge Clo. *Ink*. 5B 16
Blunt Av. *Mas M*. 4A 10
Blyth Clo. *Ches*. 4F 21
Bobbinmill La. *Ches*. 2H 21
Bodmin Way. *Ches*. 5G 13
Boland Rd. *Shef*. 1B 2
Bolehill. **6A 4**
   (Barlow)
Bolehill. **3B 24**
   (Calow)
Bole Hill. **5H 29**
   (Wingerworth)
Bole Hill. *Cal* 3A 24
Bolehill La. *Tup* 6G 29
Bolsover. **3E 27**
Bolsover Bus. Pk.
   Bsvr. 2C 26
Bolsover Castle. **2D 26**
BOLSOVER HOSPITAL.
   . . . . 2G 27
Bolsover Rd. *Mas M* 4B 10
Bolsover Rd. *Shut*. 4D 18
Bolsover Woodhouse.
   . . . . **5C 18**
Bondfield Rd. *Ink*. 3C 16
Bond St. *Stav*. 2C 16
Bonsall Ct. *Ches* *3H 13*
   (off Bowness Rd.)
Border Clo. *Clow*. 6G 19
Border La. *Clow*. 6G 19
Bottom Rd. *Wing*. 4A 30
Boughton La. *Clow*. 3H 11
Boulton Clo. *Ches*. 5E 13
Boundary Clo. *Stav* 5G 9
Bourne Clo. *Brim*. 1G 15
Bourne Mill Clo.
   Blbgh. 1F 11
Bowdon Av. *Blbgh*. 2E 11
Bower Farm Rd.
   Old W. 6D 6
Bowland Dri. *Walt* 5F 21
Bowness Clo. *Ches*. 3H 13
Bowness Clo. *Dron W*. . . . 5C 2
Bowness Rd. *Ches*. 3H 13
Bowshaw. **2D 2**
Bowshaw. *Dron*. 3D 2
Bowshaw Av. *Shef*. 1E 3
Bowshaw Clo. *Shef*. 1E 3
Bowshaw Vw. *Shef*. 1E 3
Boythorpe. **3A 22**
Boythorpe Av. *Ches*. 2A 22
Boythorpe Cres. *Ches*. . . . 3B 22
Boythorpe Mt. *Ches*. 2B 22
Boythorpe Ri. *Ches*. 2A 22
Boythorpe Rd. *Ches*. 2B 22
Bracken Av. *Heath* 5F 33
Brackendale Clo. *Brim*. . . . 3F 15
Brackendale Clo.
   Dane. 6G 35
Bracken La. *Blbgh*. 2F 11
Bradbourne Clo. *Stav*. . . . 2C 16
Bradbury Clo. *Ches*. 1A 22
Bradbury Dri. *Wing*. 2A 30
Bradgate Cft. *Ches*. 5E 23
Bradley Clo. *Brim*. 3G 15
Bradley La. *Barl*. 4A 4
Bradley Way. *Brim*. 2G 15

Bradshaw Rd. Ink 4B **16**
Bradway. **1A 2**
Bradway Grange Rd.
    Shef. 1A **2**
Bradway Rd. Shef 1A **2**
Bradwell Clo. Dron W 5A **2**
Bradwell Gro. Dane 6F **35**
Bradwell Pl. Ink 3C **16**
Braemar Clo. New W 4F **7**
Bramble Clo. Heath 5F **33**
Brambling Ct. Ches 1E **23**
Bramlyn Clo. Clow. 3H **11**
Bramlyn Ct. Clow. 3H **11**
Brampton. **1H 21**
Brampton Ct. Ches 1G **21**
Bramshill Ri. Ches. 3H **21**
Brandene Clo. Cal 1A **24**
Branksome Chine Av.
    Has 5E **23**
Branton Clo. Ches 3B **22**
Brassington La. Old T . . . 1E **35**
Brassington St.
    Clay C 4F **35**
Brearley Av. New W 5F **7**
Brearley Hall. Old W. 4E **7**
Brearley St. Old W 5E **7**
Breckland Rd. Ches 4F **21**
Breck La. Bar H 4C **8**
Brecon Clo. Ches. 5G **13**
Brendon Av. Ches 6G **13**
Brent Clo. Ches 5H **13**
Bretby Rd. Ches. 4E **13**
Bretton Av. Bsvr. 2G **27**
Bretton Clo. Ches. 5E **13**
Brewery St. Ches. 1D **22**
Briar Briggs Rd. Bsvr 1D **26**
Briar Clo. Ches. 5A **14**
Briardene Clo. Ches 5D **12**
Briar Vw. Brim. 3G **15**
Brickhouse Yd. Ches 1A **22**
Brickyard Wlk. Ches 1C **22**
Bricky Clo. Clow. 3H **11**
Bri. Bank Clo. Ches 4H **13**
Bridge St. Ches 3C **22**
Bridge St. Clay C 4E **35**
Bridge St. New T 5F **31**
Bridge St. Ind. Est.
    Clay C 4E **35**
Bridgewater St.
    New T 5E **31**
Bridge Way. Ches 5H **5**
Bridle Rd. Mas M 1H **17**
Bridle Rd. Stanf 1F **19**
Brierley Clo. Stav 1E **17**
Brierley Rd. Uns 2A **6**
Bright St. N Wing 1H **35**
Brimington. **2H 15**
Brimington Rd. Ches 6D **14**
Brimington Rd. N.
    Ches 1C **14**
    (in two parts)
Brimington Common. . . 5H **15**
Brincliffe Clo. Ches. 3F **21**
Brindley Rd. Ches 4C **14**
Brindley Way. Stav. 6F **9**
Brindwoodgate. **3A 4**
Britannia Rd. Ches 5D **22**
Broadgorse Clo. Ches . . . 5B **22**
Broadleys. Clay C. 5E **35**
Broadoaks Clo. Ches 1D **22**
Broad Pavement.
    Ches 1C **22**
Brockhill Ct. Brim 2H **15**
Brocklehurst Ct. Ches . . . 1H **21**
Brocklehurst Piece.
    Ches 2H **21**
Brockley Av. Shut 4D **18**
Brockway Clo. Dane 6F **35**
Brockwell. **6A 14**
Brockwell Ct. Ches 4H **13**
Brockwell Hill. **5H 13**
Brockwell La. Ches 4H **13**

Brockwell La. Cut 3D **12**
Brockwell Pl. Ches. 6A **14**
Brockwell Ter. Ches 6A **14**
Brockwell Wlk. Ches 5H **13**
Bromehead Way.
    Ches. 3H **13**
Brookbank Av. Ches. 6H **13**
Brookbank Rd. Clow 5G **19**
Brook Clo. Holy 5B **20**
Brooke Dri. Brim 5H **15**
Brookfield Av. Ches 2E **21**
Brookfield Pk. (Cvn. Site)
    Old T. 3A **34**
Brookfield Rd. Bsvr 4E **27**
Brookhill. Clow. 5F **19**
Brook La. Clow 5G **19**
Brooklyn Dri. Ches 6H **13**
Brookside. **2F 21**
Brookside Bar. Ches 2D **20**
Brookside Glen. Ches 2D **20**
Brooks Rd. Bar H. 4B **8**
Brook St. Clay C 4C **34**
Brook St. Ren 1A **10**
Brook Va. Ches 2A **22**
Brook Va. Clo. Barl 5B **4**
Brookview Ct. Dron 3E **3**
Brook Yd. Ches 1A **22**
Broombank Pk. Ches. 5H **5**
Broombank Pk. Ind. Est.
    Ches. 5H **5**
Broombank Rd. Ches 5G **5**
Broom Bus. Pk. Ches 5H **5**
Broom Clo. Ches 3H **13**
Broom Dri. Gras 4G **31**
Broomfield Av. Has. 5F **23**
Broom Gdns. Brim 3H **15**
Broomhill Rd. Old W 6B **6**
Broughton Rd. Ches 3H **13**
Browning Ct. Ches 1F **21**
Brown La. Coal A. 3G **3**
Brunswick St. Ches 6C **14**
Brushes, The. **4B 6**
Brushfield Rd. Ches. 5D **12**
Bryn Lea. Ches. 2E **23**
Buckden Clo. Ches 6H **13**
Buckingham Clo.
    Dron W 4B **2**
Budget La. Scar. 6H **27**
Bungalows, The.
    Ches 2D **22**
    (off Piccadilly Rd.)
Bungalows, The.
    Ches 1H **21**
    (Barker La.)
Bungalows, The.
    Ches 2C **14**
    (Brimington Rd. N.)
Bungalows, The.
    Ches 3A **14**
    (Littlemoor)
Bungalows, The. Clow . . . 4F **19**
Bungalows, The. Stav . . . 2C **16**
Bunting Clo. Walt. 3F **21**
Buntingfield La. Asvr. . . . 6A **28**
Bunting Ho. Old W 5D **6**
Burbage Clo. Dron W. . . . 4B **2**
Burbage Rd. Stav 3D **16**
Burgess Clo. Has 5F **23**
Burkitt Dri. Mas M. 5H **9**
Burley Clo. Ches 5C **22**
Burlington St. Ches 1C **22**
Burnaston Clo.
    Dron W 5A **2**
Burnbridge Rd. Old W . . . 5E **7**
Burnell St. Brim 2H **15**
Burns Clo. Ches. 5B **22**
Burns Dri. Dron. 6G **3**
Burns Dri. Gras 3G **31**
Burrs Wood Cft. Ches . . . 3F **13**
Bursden Clo. Old W. 1C **14**
Buttermere Clo. Ches . . . 3H **13**
Buttermere Dri.
    Dron. 5C **2**

Buttermilk La. Bsvr 1A **26**
Butterton Dri. Ches 5E **13**
Byron Clo. Dron. 1G **5**
Byron Clo. Gras. 3G **31**
Byron Rd. Ches 4C **22**
Byron St. Ches 3D **22**

C

Caernarvon Clo. Ches 4G **21**
Caernarvon Rd. Dron. 6F **3**
Cairn Dri. New W 4F **7**
Cairngorm Clo. New W . . . 4F **7**
Caldey Rd. Dron. 6E **3**
California La. Blbgh 1E **11**
Callywhite La. Dron 5F **3**
Calow. **2H 23**
Calow Brook Dri. Has 4G **23**
Calow Green. **4B 24**
Calow La. Has & Cal 4F **23**
Calow La. Ind. Est.
    Has. 4G **23**
Calstock Clo. Ches. 6E **13**
Calver Av.
    N Wing . . . . . . 6A **32** & 1H **35**
Calver Cres. Stav. 3D **16**
Cambrian Clo. Ches 4H **13**
Cambridge Rd. Brim 2H **15**
Camerory Way. New W . . . 3F **7**
Camlough Wlk. Ches 1D **22**
Campbell Dri. Bar H. 5A **8**
Canal M. Ches 5C **14**
Canal Wharf. Ches. 6D **14**
Cannell Clo. Clay C 4D **34**
Cantrell Clo. Brim. 2F **15**
Capel Ri. Brim 2F **15**
Capthorne Clo. Ches 5D **12**
Carlisle Clo. Ches. 5A **6**
Carlton Clo. Dane. 6F **35**
Carlton Rd. Ches 6B **22**
Carlyon Gdns. Ches 4B **22**
Carnoustie Av. Ches 4G **21**
Carpenter Av. Mas M. . . . 5H **9**
Carr La. Dron W 4A **2**
Carr La. Pal 5C **26**
Carr Vale. **4D 26**
Carr Va. Rd. Bsvr. 3D **26**
Carrwood Rd. Ches 5F **5**
Carrwood Rd. Ren. 1H **9**
Carsington Clo. Ches 5F **13**
Cartmel Clo. Dron W 5C **2**
Cartmel Cres. Ches 2H **13**
Castle Grn. Bsvr. 4F **27**
Castle La. Bsvr. 3D **26**
Castlerigg Way.
    Dron W 5C **2**
Castle St. Bsvr. 2E **27**
Castleton Gro. Ink 5B **16**
Castle Yd. Ches 2C **22**
Catchford Vw. Ches 3F **13**
Catherine Ct. Ches. 1A **22**
Catherine St. Ches 1A **22**
Caudwell Clo. New T 6F **31**
Cauldon Dri. Ches 5E **13**
Cavell Dri. Dane. 6G **35**
Cavendish Clo. Hlmwd. . . 5E **23**
Cavendish Ct. Ches 5C **14**
Cavendish Dri. Clow 5H **19**
    (in two parts)
Cavendish Pl. Bar H. 5B **8**
Cavendish Ri. Dron 6D **2**
Cavendish Rd. Bsvr. 4F **27**
Cavendish Sq. Mar L 1F **7**
Cavendish St. Ches 1C **22**
Cavendish St. Stav. 2C **16**
Cavendish St. N.
    Old W 6C **6**
Cavendish Ter. Mar L 1F **7**
Cavendish Wlk. Ches 2E **27**
Caxton Clo. New W 6F **7**
Cecil Av. Dron 4E **3**

Cecil Rd. Dron 3E **3**
Cedar Av. Ches 5H **13**
Cedar Pk. Dri. Bsvr 2G **27**
Cedar St. Holl 1A **16**
Cemetery La. Stav 1E **17**
Cemetery Rd. Ches 2E **23**
Cemetery Rd. Dane 6F **35**
Cemetery Rd. Dron 6F **3**
Cemetery Ter. Brim 3G **15**
Central Av. Ches 2A **22**
Central Clo. Uns 2A **6**
Central Dri. Cal 1H **23**
Central Dri. Has. 3E **23**
Central Dri. Wing. 3B **30**
Central Pavement.
    Ches 1C **22**
    (off Market Pl.)
Central St. Ches. 1B **22**
Central St. Hlmwd. 6D **32**
Central Ter. Ches 2D **22**
Central Wlk. Brim. 3F **15**
Chaddesden Clo.
    Dron W 5A **2**
Challands Clo. Has. 4E **23**
Challands Way. Has. 4E **23**
Chander Hill La.
    Holy 3A **20**
Chaneyfield Way.
    Ches 3F **13**
Chantrey Av. Ches. 4B **14**
Chapel Clo. Clow 5F **19**
Chapel Cotts. Mar L 1F **7**
Chapel Hill. **5G 33**
Chapel La. E. Has. 5F **23**
Chapel La. W. Ches 2G **21**
Chapel Rd. Bsvr 3D **26**
Chapel Rd. Gras 3G **31**
Chapel St. Brim. 2H **15**
Chapel St. Ches. 2C **14**
    (off Station Rd.)
Chapel St. Ches. 2C **14**
    (Brimington Rd.)
Chapel Wlk. Bsvr. 2E **27**
Chapel Way. New T 5F **31**
Chapman La. Gras. 3H **31**
Charles St. Ches 1A **22**
Charlesworth Gdns.
    Bsvr 4C **26**
    (off Charlesworth St.)
Charlesworth St.
    Bsvr 4C **26**
Chartwell Av. Wing 1H **29**
Chartwell Ri. Ches. 1A **30**
Chasecliff Clo. Ches 5H **13**
Chatsworth Av. Ches 2F **21**
Chatsworth Av. Clow. . . . 5G **19**
Chatsworth Bus. Pk.
    Ches 2A **22**
Chatsworth Clo. Bsvr 2G **27**
Chatsworth Ct. Stav 2D **16**
Chatsworth Dri.
    N Wing 2H **35**
Chatsworth Pl. Dron W . . . 4B **2**
Chatsworth Rd. Ches 2D **20**
CHATSWORTH SUITE. (BMI)
    . . . . 1G **23**
Chaucer Dri. Dron 1G **5**
Chaucer Rd. Ches 2B **14**
Chavery Rd. Clay C 4G **35**
Cheadle Av. Ches. 5G **13**
Cheadle Clo. Ches. 4H **13**
Cheadle Wlk. Ches. 5H **13**
Cheetham Av. Uns 3A **6**
Chelmsford Way.
    Bar H 4B **8**
Chepstow Clo. Ches 4B **22**
Chepstow Gdns. Ches . . . 5B **22**
Cherry Tree Clo. Bsvr. . . . 3F **27**
Cherry Tree Clo. Clow . . . 6F **19**
Cherry Tree Dri. Duck . . . 6G **17**
Cherry Tree Gro.
    Mas M 5A **10**

Cherry Tree Gro.
   N Wing 3H **35**
Chertsey Clo. Ches 4B **22**
Cherwell Clo. Brim. 1G **15**
Chesterfield. 1C **22**
**CHESTERFIELD & NORTH
DERBYSHIRE ROYAL
HOSPITAL.** 1G **23**
Chesterfield Av.
   New W 5G **7**
Chesterfield Crematorium.
   Brim 4F **15**
Chesterfield Golf Course.
   . . . . 5A **22**
Chesterfield Inner Relief Rd.
   Ches 6A **6**
Chesterfield Mus. & Art Gallery.
   . . . . 1D **22**
Chesterfield Rd.
   Ark T & Duck 2B **24**
Chesterfield Rd.
   Blbgh 3E **11**
Chesterfield Rd. Bsvr 5C **18**
Chesterfield Rd. Brim 3F **15**
Chesterfield Rd. Cal 2G **23**
Chesterfield Rd. Dron 5E **3**
Chesterfield Rd. Gras 5H **31**
Chesterfield Rd.
   Holl & Stav 2A **16**
Chesterfield Rd.
   Temp N 3C **32**
Chesterfield Rd. S.
   Shef 1E **3**
Chesterfield Small Bus. Cen.
   Ches 3C **14**
   (off Pottery La. W.)
Chesterfield Trad. Est.
   Ches 5G **5**
Chester Ho. Ches 1A **14**
Chester St. Ches 1A **22**
Chesterton Clo. Brim 6H **15**
Chestnut Clo. Dron 6G **3**
Chestnut Dri. Clow 4H **11**
Cheviot Way. Ches. 5G **13**
Chigwell Way. Bar H 5B **8**
Chiltern Clo. Ches 6G **13**
Chiltern Clo. Gras 3H **31**
Chiltern Ct. Ches 6G **13**
   (off Brendon Av.)
Chiltern Wlk. Gras 3H **31**
Chiverton Clo. Dron 4E **3**
Church Av. Dane 5G **35**
Church Clo. Clow. 6G **19**
Church Clo. Ink 3C **16**
Church Clo. N Wing 2C **30**
Church Farm M.
   Temp N 3B **32**
Church Hill. 2G **35**
Churchland Av.
   Hlmwd 6D **32**
Church La. Cal 1H **23**
Church La. Ches 1C **22**
Church La. Clow 6G **19**
Church La. Heath 3H **33**
   (in two parts)
Church La. N Wing 3H **35**
Church La. Temp N 3B **32**
Church La. N. Old W 5C **6**
Church Meadows. Cal . . . 1H **23**
Church Meadows.
   N Wing 3H **35**
Church Paddock.
   N Wing 3H **35**
Church Rd. Stanf 4E **19**
   (in two parts)
Churchside. Cal 1H **23**
Churchside. Has 6F **23**
Churchside La. Has 6F **23**
Church St. Blbgh 1F **11**
Church St. Bsvr 3E **27**
Church St. Brim. 3G **15**
Church St. Cal 1H **23**
Church St. Clow 6F **19**

Church St. Dron 5E **3**
Church St. Stav 6E **9**
Church St. Uns 1A **6**
Church St. N. Old W 5C **6**
Church St. S. Ches 5B **22**
   (in two parts)
Church St. W. Ches 2G **21**
Church Vw. Blbgh 1E **11**
Church Vw. Ches 2G **21**
Church Vw. Clow 6G **19**
Church Wlk. Ches 1C **22**
   (off Stephenson Pl.)
Church Wlk. New W. 4F **7**
Church Way. Ches 1C **22**
Churston Rd. Ches 1H **21**
Circular Rd. Has 4D **22**
Circular Rd. Stav 2D **16**
Clarence Rd. Ches 1B **22**
Clarence St. Ches 1B **22**
Clarendon Rd. Ink 4C **16**
Clarkson Av. Ches 4B **22**
Clay Cross. 4E **35**

**CLAY CROSS COMMUNITY
HOSPITAL.** 4F **35**
Clay Cross Countryside Cen.
   . . . . 5E **35**
Clay La. Clay C 6D **34**
Clay Pit Way. Blbgh 2G **11**
Clayton St. Ches 2D **22**
Cleveland Way. Ches 6F **13**
Cliff Hill. Clow 5G **11**
Clifford Clo. Ches 2F **21**
Clifton Av. Blbgh 1E **11**
Clifton St. Ches 1A **22**
Clough, The. Ches 3G **23**
Clowne. 5F **19**
Clowne Rd. Blbgh 2F **11**
Clowne Rd. Shut 3D **18**
Clubmill Ter. Ches 6A **14**
Clumber Clo. Clow 5G **19**
Clumber Pl. Ink 4C **16**
Clune St. Clow 4H **19**
Coal Aston. 2G **3**
Cobden Rd. Ches 6B **14**
Cobnar Dri. Ches 2H **13**
Cobnar Wood Clo.
   Ches 5F **5**
Cock Alley. 3A **24**
College Av. Stav 1D **16**
College Vw. Clow 6F **19**
Colliers Trek. Blbgh 3G **11**
Colliers Way. Clay C 4D **34**
Colliery Clo. Stav 1F **17**
Collins Yd. Dron 5E **3**
   (off Mill La.)
Collishaw Clo. Has 4E **23**
Colton Clo. Ches 1A **14**
Common La. Cut 2C **12**
Commonpiece Rd.
   Clay C 5F **35**
Common Side. 5B **4**
Commonside Rd. Barl . . . 6A **4**
Compass Cres. Old W . . . 5E **7**
Compton St. Ches 1B **22**
Compton St. Hlmwd 5E **33**
Conalan Av. Shef 1A **2**
Conduit Rd. Bsvr 4F **27**
Coney Grn. Rd.
   Clay C 4G **35**
Coniston Dri. Clay C 6D **34**
Coniston Rd. Ches 2H **13**
Coniston Rd. Dron W 6B **2**
Coniston Way. Ches 2H **13**
Connelly Ct. Ches 1A **22**
Constable Clo. Dron 5C **2**
Cooke Clo. Old T 2D **34**
Coole Well Clo. Stav 2D **16**
Co-operative Cotts.
   Pool 3G **17**
Copenhagen Rd.
   Clay C 4G **35**
Coppice Clo. Has 6F **23**
Coral Way. Clay C 4F **35**

Corbriggs. 1H **31**
Cordwell Av. Ches 2G **13**
Cordwell Clo. Stav 2D **16**
Cornfield Clo. Ash 5E **13**
Cornhill Clo. Bsvr 2F **27**
Cornwall Av. Brim 2H **15**
Cornwall Clo. Brim 2H **15**
Cornwall Dri. Brim. 2H **15**
Cornwall Dri. Gras. 3H **31**
Coronation Rd. Brim 2G **15**
Corporation St. Ches 1D **22**
   (in two parts)
Corve Way. Ches 5D **12**
Cotswold Clo. Ches 5G **13**
Cotswold Dri. Gras 3G **31**
Cottage Clo. Pool 2G **17**
Cottam Dri. Blbgh 2G **11**
Cotterhill La. Brim 3G **15**
Cotton Mill Hill. Holy 5B **20**
Cotton St. Bsvr 3E **27**
Coupe La.
   Clay C & Old T 3C **34**
Coupland Clo. Old W 4E **7**
Court Pl. Stav 2C **16**
Court Vw. Clow 6F **19**
Cow La. Brim. 1G **15**
Cowley. 1B **4**
Cowley Clo. Ches 1D **22**
Cowley La. Holm 6A **2**
Cowpingle La. Brim 1G **15**
   (in two parts)
Cowsell Dri. Dane 6G **35**
Craggon Dri. New W 4F **7**
Craggs Dri. Clow 6F **19**
Craggs Rd. Bsvr 2E **27**
Craglands Gro. Ches 5E **13**
Cragside Clo. Ches 1E **23**
Cranborne Rd. Ches 3A **14**
Cranleigh Rd. Mas M 6H **9**
Craven Rd. Ches 5B **14**
Crescent Rd. Holy 5B **20**
Crescent, The. Blbgh 2G **11**
Crescent, The. Brim 3E **15**
Crescent, The. Clay C . . . 6E **35**
Crescent, The. Holy 5B **20**
Creswell Rd. Clow 4F **19**
Creswick Clo. Ches 4F **21**
Crich Pl. N Wing 2H **35**
Crich Rd. Ink 3C **16**
Crich Vw. Bsvr 4F **27**
Cricket Vw. Clow 6H **11**
Croft Lea. Dron W 4A **2**
Crofton Clo. Dron 5D **2**
Crofton Ri. Dron 5D **2**
Croft Vw. Clow. 6G **19**
Croft Vw. Ink 4C **16**
Cromarty Ri. Dron W 4B **2**
Cromdale Av. New W 4F **7**
Cromford Ct. Ches 3H **13**
   (off Bowness Rd.)
Cromford Dri. Stav 2B **16**
Cromford Rd. Clay C 3C **34**
Crompton Rd. Stav 6F **9**
Cromwell Rd. Bsvr 4F **27**
Cromwell Rd. Ches 6B **14**
Cropston Clo. Ches 5E **23**
Cross La. Coal A 1G **3**
   (Dyche La.)
Cross La. Coal A 3G **3**
   (Green La.)
Cross La. Dron. 5E **3**
Cross London St.
   New W 5F **7**
Cross St. Bsvr 4G **27**
Cross St. Brim. 2G **15**
Cross St. Ches. 6B **14**
Cross St. Clay C. 5E **35**
Cross St. Gras. 3H **31**
Cross St. N Wing. 2G **35**
Cross Wellington St.
   New W 5F **7**
Crow La. App. 1A **6**
Crow La. Ches. 1D **22**

Crown Clo. New W 5F **7**
Crown Rd. Ches. 5C **14**
Crown St. Clow 6F **19**
Cruck Clo. Dron W 4B **2**
Cundy Rd. Bsvr 1E **27**
Cunliffe St. Coal A 2G **3**
Curbar Clo. N Wing 6A **32**
Curbar Curve. Ink 4B **16**
Curzon Av. Dron 6D **2**
Cuttholme Clo. Ches 6F **13**
Cuttholme Rd. Ches 6F **13**
Cuttholme Way. Ches 6G **13**
Cutthorpe. 3D **12**
Cutthorpe Common End.
   . . . . 3E **13**
Cutthorpe Grange.
   Ches 3E **13**
Cutthorpe Rd. Ches 3D **12**

D

Dade Av. Ink. 4B **16**
Dalbury Rd. Dron W 5A **2**
Dale Bank Cres.
   New W 5F **7**
Dale Clo. Stav 2C **16**
Dale Cres. New T 5E **31**
Dale Rd. Dron 6F **3**
Dale Rd. New T 5E **31**
Dalewood Clo. Ches 3G **23**
Dalvey Way. New W 3F **7**
Damon Dri. Brim. 2H **15**
Damsbrook Dri. Clow. . . . 6F **19**
Damsbrook La. Clow 1H **19**
Damson Cft. Holl 6A **8**
Danbury Clo. Gras. 3G **31**
Danby Av. Old W 6D **6**
Danesmoor. 5F **35**
Danesmoor Ind. Est.
   Dane. 5H **35**
Dark La. Brim 6G **15**
Dark La. Cal. 2H **23**
Darley Clo. Stav 1E **17**
Darley Rd. Asvr 4A **28**
Darwent Rd. Ches 4E **15**
Darwin Av. Ches 5A **14**
Darwin Rd. Ches 6B **14**
Darwood La. Bsvr 4E **27**
Davenport Rd. New T. . . . 6E **31**
Davey Ct. Bsvr. 1D **26**
Davian Way. Ches 4A **22**
Davids Dri. Wing 2A **30**
Deben Clo. Ches 4G **21**
Deepdale Clo. Stav. 5E **9**
Deepdale Rd. Bsvr. 1D **26**
Deepsic La. Ark T 3C **24**
Deerlands Rd. Ches 1F **21**
Deerlands Rd. Wing 3B **30**
Deerleap La. Clay C 5A **34**
Deerpark Cres. Wing 3B **30**
Deincourt Cres.
   N Wing 6H **31**
Dell, The. Ches 1F **21**
Delph Bank. Ches 4A **22**
Delves Clo. Ches 3H **21**
Denby Rd. Ink 3C **16**
Denham St. Clay C 5F **35**
Derby Rd.
   Ches & Wing 5C **22**
Derby Rd.
   Old T & Clay C 1D **34**
Derwent Clo. Dron 3F **3**
Derwent Cres. Ches. 3H **13**
Derwent Ho. Ches 3H **13**
   (off Ullverston Rd.)
Derwent Pl. Clay C 3C **34**
Derwent Rd. Dron 3F **3**
Derwent Vw. Mas M 5A **10**
Devizes Clo. Ches 4B **22**
Devon Clo. Gras 4H **31**
Devon Dri. Brim. 2H **15**

Devon Pk. Vw. *Brim* 2H **15**
Devonshire Av. E. *Has* 4E **23**
Devonshire Av. N.
  New W 4F **7**
Devonshire Clo. *Ches* 2B **14**
Devonshire Clo. *Dron* 6D **2**
Devonshire Clo. *Stav* 6E **9**
Devonshire Cotts.
  Bar H 5B **8**
Devonshire Ct. *Brim* 3F **15**
Devonshire Pk. *Brim* . . . 2G **15**
Devonshire Rd. E.
  Has 4E **23**
Devonshire Rd. N.
  New W 5F **7**
Devonshire St. *Brim* 2G **15**
Devonshire St. Ches *1C* **22**
  (off Holywell St.)
Devonshire St. *Stav* 6E **9**
Devonshire Ter.
  Hlmwd 5E **33**
Devonshire Vs. *Bar H* 5C **8**
Devonshire Vs. Ches *2B* **14**
  (off Occupation Rd.)
Devonshire Vs. Hlmwd . . . *6E* **33**
  (off Heath Rd.)
Devonshire Way.
  Clow 5G **19**
Dickens Dri. *Hlmwd* 5D **32**
Dickenson Rd. *Ches* 3D **22**
Didcot Clo. *Ches* 4B **22**
Dingle Bank. *Cal* 3G **23**
Dingle La. *Cal* 3G **23**
  (in two parts)
Discovery Way.
  Whit M 1C **14**
Division St. *Stav* 2C **16**
Dixon Cft. *New W* 4F **7**
Dixon Rd. *Ches* 2D **22**
Dobbin La. *Barl* 3A **4**
Dobson Pl. *Ink* 4B **16**
Dock Wlk. *Ches* 2A **22**
Dore & Totley Golf Course.
  . . . . 1B **2**
Dorothy Va. *Ches* 6G **13**
Dorset Av. *Brim* 2H **15**
Dorset Clo. *Brim* 1H **15**
Dorset Dri. *Brim* 2H **15**
Douglas Rd. *Ches* 4E **15**
Dovedale Av. *Ink* 5B **16**
Dovedale Ct. *Ches* 3A **14**
Doveridge Clo. *Old W* 6C **6**
Dowdeswell St. *Ches* 6C **14**
Downlands. *Brim* 3F **15**
Drake Ter. *Brim* 2E **15**
Draycott Pl. *Dron W* 6B **2**
Draycott Rd. *N Wing* . . . 1H **35**
Dronfield. 5E **3**
Dronfield Ind. Est.
  Dron 5G **3**
Dronfield Woodhouse. . . . 5B **2**
Drury La. *Coal A* 3G **3**
Dryden Av. *Ches* 4C **22**
Duckmanton. 2B **24**
  (Calow)
Duckmanton. 5G **17**
  (Inkersall Green)
Duckmanton Moor. . . . 3E **25**
Duckmanton Rd.
  Duck. 5G **17**
Duewell Ct. *Bar H* 5B **8**
Dukeries Ct. *Clow* 6G **19**
Dukes Clo. *Hlmwd* 5E **33**
Dukes Dri. *Ches* 4A **14**
Duke St. *Ches* 2C **14**
Duke St. *Clow* 5H **19**
  (in two parts)
Duke St. *Stav* 6E **9**
Dumbles Rd. *Bsvr* 3D **26**
Dumble Wood Grange.
  Ches 3G **13**
Dundonald Rd. *Ches* 3C **22**
Dunshill Wlk. *Clay C* 4G **35**

Dunston. 2H **13**
Dunston Ct. *Ches.* 1B **14**
Dunston La. *Ches* 1H **13**
Dunston Pl. *Ches.* 1B **14**
Dunston Rd. *Ches* 2E **13**
Dunston Trad. Est.
  Ches 6A **6**
Dunvegan Av. *Dane* . . . 6G **35**
Durham Av. *Gras* 4H **31**
Durham Av. *New W* 5F **7**
Durham Clo. *New W* 5F **7**
Durley Chine Dri. *Has* . . . 4E **23**
Durrant Rd. *Ches* 1C **22**
Dye Works Yd. *Holy.* 6B **20**
Dykes Clo. *Bsvr* 2E **27**
Dymond Clo. *Gras* 3H **31**

E

Easedale Clo. *Ches* 5D **12**
East Av. *Stanf.* 1F **19**
East Cres. *Duck.* 4G **17**
Eastern Av. *Bsvr.* 4F **27**
Eastfield Rd. *Dron* 6G **3**
Eastleigh Ct. *Has* 4F **23**
Eastmoor Rd. *Brim* 6H **15**
E. Side Clo. *Ches.* 2D **14**
E. Side Rd. *Ches* 2D **14**
East St. *Clay C* 4F **35**
East St. *Clow* 4H **19**
East St. *Ren.* 1H **9**
East St. *Scar* 6H **27**
East Vw. *Bsvr* 5F **27**
East Vw. *Ches* 2C **22**
Eastwood Clo. *Has* 4F **23**
Eastwood Dri. *Cal* 2B **24**
Eastwood Pk. Apartments
  Ches. 5E **23**
Eastwood Pk. Dri.
  Has 4F **23**
Eckington Rd. *Coal A.* . . . 2G **3**
Eckington Rd. *New W* 3F **7**
Eckington Rd. *Stav.* 5F **9**
Edale Ct. *Ches* 3A **14**
Edale Rd. *Mas M.* 5A **10**
Edensor Clo. *N Wing* . . . 2H **35**
Edensor Ct. *Stav* 2C **16**
Eden St. *Wing* 3A **30**
Edinburgh Ct. Ches *6B* **14**
  (off Highfield Rd.)
Edinburgh Ct. *Wing* 2A **30**
Edinburgh Rd. *Ches.* 5B **14**
Edinburgh Rd. *Wing* . . . 2A **30**
Edmund Av. *Shef.* 1A **2**
Edmund Clo. *Shef.* 1B **2**
Edmund St. *Ches.* 2B **14**
Edward St. *Stav.* 2C **16**
Edward Wlk. New T *5F* **31**
  (off Queen Victoria Rd.)
Edwin Av. *Ches* 4H **21**
Egerton Rd. *Dron.* 4F **3**
Egstow. 4F **35**
Egstow Pl. *Clay C.* 4F **35**
Egstow St. *Clay C.* 4F **35**
Elder Way. *Ches.* 1C **22**
Eldon St. *Clay C* 4E **35**
Elgin Clo. *Ches* 5G **21**
Eliot Clo. *Brim* 5H **15**
Elkstone Rd. *Ches.* 5E **13**
Elliott Dri. *Ink.* 4C **16**
Elm Clo. *Bsvr.* 3G **27**
Elm Clo. *Ches* 3B **14**
Elm Gro. *Clay C* 5F **35**
Elm Lodge Farm Clo.
  Ches 3B **14**
Elm Pl. *Ches.* 2A **22**
Elm St. *Holl* 1H **15**
Elm St. *Temp N* 2B **32**
Elmton Clo. *Clow.* 6G **19**
Elmton La. *Bsvr* 2F **27**
Elm Tree Cres. *Dron.* 3E **3**

Elm Tree Dri. *Wing.* 2B **30**
Elmwood Ho. *Holl* 2A **16**
Elton Clo. *N Wing* 3H **35**
Elton St. *Ches.* 2C **22**
Elton Vw. *Stav.* 2D **16**
Elvaston Clo. *Dron W* . . . 5A **2**
Elvaston Rd. *N Wing* . . . 2H **35**
Elvin Way. *New T.* 6E **31**
Emmetfield Clo. *Ches* . . . 4B **22**
Emmett Carr. 1A **10**
Emmett Carr Clo. *Ren* . . . 1A **10**
Endowood Rd. *Ches* . . . 4E **21**
Enfield Rd. *Ches* 5B **14**
Ennerdale Clo. *Dron W* . . 5C **2**
Ennerdale Cres. *Ches* . . 3G **13**
Enterprise Dri.
  Hlmwd 5D **32**
Erin Rd. *Pool & Duck.* . . . 2F **17**
Errington Rd. *Ches* 4H **21**
Eskdale Clo. *Bsvr.* 3D **26**
Eskdale Clo. *Dron W* . . . 5C **2**
Ettrick Clo. *Ches* 5G **13**
Etwall Clo. *Ches.* 4E **13**
Everett Clo. *Brim.* 3G **15**
Excalibur Way. *Ches.* . . 1D **22**
Eyam Clo. *N Wing* 6A **32**
Eyre Gdns. *Ches* 6B **14**
Eyre St. *Clay C.* 4E **35**
Eyre St. E. *Ches.* 5E **23**

F

Fabric Vw. *Hlmwd* 6D **32**
Factory St. *Ches* 2H **21**
Fairburn Cft. Cres.
  Blbgh 2F **11**
Fair Clo. *Ches* 6A **14**
Fairfield Clo. *Brim* 2F **15**
Fairfield Ct. *Ash.* 6D **12**
Fairfield Dri. *Ash* 6D **12**
Fairfield Dri. *N Wing* . . . 2H **35**
Fairfield Rd. *Bsvr.* 4E **27**
Fairfield Rd. *Ches* 6B **14**
Fairford Clo. *Ches* 5B **22**
Fair Vw. *Ches.* 6A **14**
Fairview Rd. *Dron* 3E **3**
Fairways, The. *Dane* . . . 5G **35**
Fair Winds Clo. *Dron* . . . 5E **3**
Falcon Ri. *Dron* 3H **3**
Falcon Rd. *Dron* 3G **3**
Falcon Yd. Ches. *1C* **22**
  (off Low Pavement)
Falkland Ri. *Dron* 6E **3**
Fallowfield Rd. *New W* . . . 5F **7**
Fan Rd. *Stav.* 1F **17**
Fan Rd. Ind. Est. *Stav* . . . 1E **17**
Fanshaw Bank. *Dron* . . . 5E **3**
Fanshaw Rd. *Dron* 4F **3**
Far La. *Barl* 5A **4**
Farm Clo. *Ches* 6B **22**
Farm Clo. *Coal A* 2F **3**
Farmfields Clo. *Bsvr* . . . 1C **26**
Farm Vw. *New T.* 6F **31**
Farndale Av. *Walt* 4F **21**
Farndale Rd. *Stav.* 4E **9**
Farnon Clo. *Ches* 3D **22**
Farnsworth Ct. *Has* 4F **23**
Farnsworth St. *Has* 4E **23**
Farwater Clo. *Dron.* 6E **3**
Farwater La. *Dron.* 5D **2**
Fawn Clo. *Wing* 3B **30**
Featherbed La. *Bsvr.* . . . 5E **19**
Felkin St. *Ches.* 1D **22**
Fenland Way. *Ches.* . . . 4A **22**
Fern Av. *Stav* 2C **16**
Fern Clo. *Heath* 5F **33**
Ferndale Clo. *Coal A* 3H **3**
Ferndale Ri. *Coal A* 3H **3**
Ferndale Rd. *Coal A* 3H **3**
Fernwood Clo. *Has* 5G **23**
Field Clo. *Dron W* 4A **2**

Fieldfare Ho. *Old W* 5D **6**
Fieldhead Way. *Ches* . . . 4G **13**
Field Vw. *Ches.* 5C **22**
Field Vw. *Clow.* 6G **19**
Fieldview Pl. *Ches.* 4G **13**
Fir St. *Holl* 1B **16**
Firthwood Av. *Coal A* 3H **3**
Firthwood Clo. *Coal A* . . . 3H **3**
Firthwood Rd. *Coal A* . . . 3H **3**
Firvale Rd. *Walt* 4F **21**
Fisher Clo. *Ches.* 5B **22**
Fishponds Clo. *Wing* . . . 3C **30**
Five Pits Trail. *Hlmwd* . . . 6E **33**
Five Pits Trail.
  N Wing 5A **32**
Flamsteed Cres. *Ches* . . . 4C **14**
Flaxpiece Rd. *Clay C* . . . 5E **35**
Fletcher Av. *Dron* 5E **3**
Flintson Av. *New W* 4F **7**
Florence Clo. *Ches.* 6B **22**
Florence Rd. *Clay C* 4F **35**
Florence Rd. *Wing.* 2A **30**
Foljambe Av. *Ches.* 4H **21**
Foljambe Rd. *Brim.* 6B **22**
Foljambe Rd. *Ches.* 1B **22**
Foolow Av. *Ches* 3B **22**
Foolow Ct. *Ches.* 3B **22**
Ford Clo. *Dron.* 5D **2**
Ford St. *New T.* 1F **35**
Forest Ct. *Blbgh* 2F **11**
Forrester's La. *Coal A* . . . 2G **3**
Forth Av. *Dron W.* 4B **2**
Foston Dri. *Ches* 5F **13**
Foundry St. *Ches.* 2C **14**
Foundry St. Ind. Est.
  Ches *2C* **14**
  (off Foundry St.)
Foundry, The. *Ches.* 2D **22**
Fowler St. *Old W* 6B **6**
Foxbrook Clo. *Ash.* 5D **12**
Foxbrook Ct. *Ches* 4F **21**
Foxbrook Dri. *Ches* 3F **21**
Foxcote Way. *Walt* 4F **21**
Foxglove Clo. *Cal.* 1A **24**
Foxley Oaks. *Old W* 1D **14**
Fox's Pl. *Ches* 2H **21**
Foxstone Clo. *Stav* 2D **16**
Foxwood Clo. *Ches* 1A **14**
Foxwood Clo. *Has* 6F **23**
Foxwood Ind. Pk.
  Ches 1B **14**
Foxwood Rd. *Ches.* 6A **6**
Foxwood Way. *Ches.* 6A **6**
Foyers Way. *Ches* 1D **22**
Frances Dri. *Wing* 2A **30**
Francis Clo. *Brim* 3F **15**
Franklyn Dri. *Stav.* 5F **9**
Franklyn Rd. *Ches* 6A **14**
Frecheville St. *Stav* 1D **16**
Frederick St. *Gras* 3G **31**
Freebirch Vw. *Ches* 3F **13**
Freshwaters
  Hlmwd 5D **32**
Freydon Way. *Cal.* 1A **24**
Friston Clo. *Ches.* 5B **22**
Frithall La. *Holy* 2A **20**
Froggatt Clo. *Ink* 4C **16**
Fulford Clo. *Ches.* 4G **21**
Fuller Dri. *Ches* 4E **15**
Furnace Clo. *Gras* 4G **31**
Furnace Hill. *Ches* 2A **22**
Furnace Hill. *Clay C* 3F **35**
Furnace Hillock Way.
  Gras 1G **31**
Furnace La. *Barl* 5D **4**
Furnace La. *Brim.* 4H **15**
Future Wlk. *Ches.* 1B **22**

G

Gables Clo. *Hlmwd* 6D **32**

Gainsborough Rd.
Dron 6C 2
Gallery La. Holy 5A 20
Gander La. Blbgh 3F 11
Gapsick La. Clow 5H 19
Garden Av. Ren 1H 9
Garden Clo. New W 5F 7
Gardeners Ct. Bsvr. 2F 27
Gardom Clo.
Dron W. 5B 2
Garret Grn. Dane 6G 35
Garret La. Dane 6F 35
Garth Way. Dron 5D 2
Garth Way Clo. Dron 5D 2
Gatefield Clo. Ches 4G 13
Gateland La. Dron 3C 4
Gelderd Pl. Dron 6E 3
Gentshill. 6G 35
Gentshill Av. Dane 6G 35
George Percival Pl.
Clay C 4C 34
George St. Brim. 2G 15
George St. N Wing 1G 35
George St. Old W. 6B 6
Gerard Clo. Ches 3G 21
Gilbert Av. Ches 4H 21
Gill's La. Gras 4G 31
Gipsy La. Old W 1D 14
Glade Clo. Ches 5A 14
Glade, The. Ches 1H 21
Gladstone Rd. Ches 6B 14
Gladwin Gdns. Ches 4H 21
Glasshouse La. New W 3F 7
Glebe Clo. Hlmwd 6D 32
Glebe Ct. Old W 6C 6
Glebe Gdns. N Wing 3H 35
Glebe, The. Old W 6C 6
    (off Glebe Way, The)
Glebe Vw. Blbgh. 2F 11
Glebe Way, The. Old W . . . 6C 6
Gledhill Clo. Dron. 5E 3
Glenavon Clo. New W 3F 7
Glencoe Way. Ches. 6F 13
Gleneagles Clo. Ches 4G 21
Glenfield Cres. Ches 3B 14
Glenmore Clo. Ink 5B 16
Glenthorne Clo. Ches. 2G 21
Glossop's Cft. Old W 6D 6
Gloucester Av. Ches. 4B 14
Gloucester Rd. Ches 5B 14
Glumangate. Ches 1C 22
Goldcrest Ho. Old W 5D 6
Gomersal La. Dron 5E 3
Goodman Ct. Cal 1A 24
Gorman Clo. Ches. 2A 14
Gorse Bank. Heath 4F 33
Gorse Valley Rd. Has. 5G 23
Gorse Valley Way.
Has 5G 23
Gorsey Brigg. Dron W 5B 2
Gosforth Clo. Dron 5D 2
Gosforth Cres. Dron 5D 2
Gosforth Dri. Dron 5B 2
Gosforth Grn. Dron 5D 2
Gosforth La. Dron 5D 2
Gower Cres. Ches 5G 13
Goyt Side Rd. Ches 2H 21
Goyt Ter. Ches 2A 22
Grampian Cres. Ches 6F 13
Granary Clo. Ches 3E 13
Grange Av. Dron W 5C 2
Grange La. Barl 1A 12
Grangemill Pl. Stav 2C 16
Grange Pk. Av. Brim 6H 15
Grange, The. Ash 6D 12
Grange Wlk. Gras 4G 31
Grangewood Rd.
Ches 5B 22
Gransden Way. Ches 4G 21
Granville Clo. Has. 4F 23
Grasmere Av. Clay C 5D 34
Grasmere Clo. Ches 3H 13
Grasmere Rd. Dron W 5B 2

Grasscroft Cvn. Site.
New W 3E 7
Grasscroft Clo. Ches 4H 13
Grasshill. 2G 31
Grassmoor. 3G 31
Grassmoor Country Pk.
. . . . 2H 31
Grassmoor Golf Course.
. . . . 2G 31
Gratton Ct. Stav 5F 9
Grayshott Wlk. Ches 4B 22
Gray St. Clow 5G 19
Gt. Common Clo.
Blbgh. 2F 11
Great Croft. Dron W. 4B 2
Greenacres Clo. Dron 1G 5
Greenaway Dri. Bsvr 4D 26
Greenbank Dri. Ches 6G 13
Green Clo. Ink 4C 16
Green Clo. Uns 2A 6
Green Cross. Dron 4F 3
Greendale Av. Holy. 4C 20
Greendale Ct. Dron. 4F 3
Greendale Shop. Cen.
Dron 4F 3
Green Farm Clo.
Ches 4G 13
Greengate Clo. Ches 2G 21
Green Glen. Ches. 2G 21
Greenhill Parkway.
Shef 1B 2
Greenland Clo.
N Wing 1H 35
Green La. Ches. 6F 15
Green La. Cut. 3C 12
Green La. Dron. 5F 3
Green La. New T 5F 31
Green Lea. Dron W 4A 2
Greenside Av. Ches 3B 14
Greenside Clo. Clow 4G 11
Green St. Old W. 6C 6
Green, The. Clow 5F 19
Green, The. Has 5E 23
Green, The. N Wing 1H 35
Green Way. Wing 4E 31
Greenways. Ches. 4G 21
Gregory Clo. Brim 2F 15
Gregory La. Brim 1F 15
Gresley Rd. Shef 1C 2
Gresley Wlk. Shef 1C 2
Griffen Clo. Stav. 2E 17
Grindlow Av. Ches 3B 22
Grindon Clo. Ches 5G 13
Grinton Wlk. Ches 4B 22
Grisedale Wlk. Dron W . . . 5C 2
Grove Farm Clo. Brim 3G 15
Grove Gdns. Brim 6H 15
Grove La. Old Br 6A 12
Grove Rd. Brim 5G 15
Grove Rd. Ches 3C 14
Grove St. Has. 4E 23
Grove, The. Pool 2G 15
Grove Way. Brim 5H 15
Grundy Rd. Clay C 5E 35
Guildford Av. Ches. 4H 21
Guildford Clo. Dane. 5G 35
Guildford La. Dane 5G 35

H

Hackney La. Barl 6D 4
Haddon Av. Clow 5H 19
Haddon Clo. Ches 2G 21
Haddon Clo. Dron 4F 3
Haddon Pl. Stav. 2D 16
Haddon Rd. N Wing. 6A 32
Hady. 2F 23
Hady Cres. Ches 2E 23
Hady Hill. Ches 2D 22
Hady La. Ches 2F 23
Hagg Hill. New T 5G 31

Hague La. Ren 1G 9
Halcyon App. Wing 4E 31
Haldane Cres. Bsvr 2D 26
Halesworth Clo. Ches. 4F 21
Halfacre La. Uns 6H 3
Half Cft. Brim. 3H 15
Hallam Ct. Dron. 6E 3
Hall Bungalows.
Wing 3C 30
Hall Clo. Cut. 2C 12
Hall Clo. Dron W 4A 2
Hall Dri. Sut S 6G 25
Hall Farm Clo. Has 5F 23
Hall Farm Cotts.
Sut S 6G 25
Hallfield Clo. Wing. 2D 30
Hallflash La. Cal. 4A 24
Hall La. Stav 4C 8
Hallowes. 6G 3
Hallowes Ct. Dron 5F 3
Hallowes Dri. Dron. 6F 3
Hallowes Golf Course.
. . . . 1F 5
Hallowes La. Dron 5F 3
Hallowes Ri. Dron 6G 3
Hall Rd. Brim. 3G 15
Hall's Row. Ches 2H 21
Hall Ter. Clay C 5F 35
Hall Vw. Ches. 4A 14
Hall Wlk. New T 5F 31
Halton Clo. Ches 1A 14
Hambledon Clo.
Ches 5G 13
Hambleton Av.
N Wing 2H 35
Hamill Clo. N Wing 1H 35
Hampton St. Ches 5F 23
Hanbury Clo. Ches. 5E 13
Hanbury Clo. Dron. 5D 2
Handby St. Has 4F 23
Handley St. New W 4F 7
Handley La. Clay C. 6C 34
Handley Rd. Mar L 2F 7
Handley Rd. New W. 4F 7
Harcourt Clo. Ches. 5E 23
Hardhurst. 2A 6
Hardhurst Rd. Uns. 3A 6
Hardie Pl. Stav. 2D 16
Hardwick Av. New W 5F 7
Hardwick Clo. Clow 5H 19
Hardwick Clo. Dron 4F 3
Hardwick Clo. Hlmwd 6E 33
Hardwick Ct. Stav 6E 9
    (off Devonshire St.)
Hardwick Dri. Ark T. 2D 24
Hardwick St. Ches. 6C 14
Hardwicks Yd. Ches. 2A 22
Hardwick Vw. Rd.
Hlmwd. 5F 33
Harehill Cres. Wing 2H 29
Harehill Rd. Ches 5B 22
Harewood Cres. Old T 2C 34
Harewood Rd. Holy 1A 28
Harlesthorpe. 4F 19
Harlesthorpe Av.
Clow 4G 19
Harlesthorpe La. Clow. . . . 4F 19
Harper Hill. 2E 29
Harperhill Clo. Ches. 5B 22
Harport Dri. Dane 6G 35
Hartfield Clo. Has 5D 22
Hartington Ct. Clow. 5H 19
Hartington Ct. Dron 4F 3
Hartington Ind. Est.
Stav. 4E 9
Hartington Rd. Ches 2E 23
Hartington Rd. Dron. 4F 3
Hartington Vw. Ches 4A 14
Hartland Way. Old W 1C 14
Hartside Clo. Ches. 5H 13
Harvest Way. Ash. 5E 13
Harvey Ct. Bsvr 2D 26
Harvey Rd. Ches 2G 23

Haslam Ct. Bsvr. 2D 26
Haslam Ct. Ches 6C 14
Hasland. 5F 23
Hasland By-Pass.
Ches & Has 3D 22
Hasland Green. 5E 23
Hasland La. Cal 4A 24
Hasland Rd. Ches 3D 22
    (in two parts)
Hassocky La.
Temp N & Cal 1B 32
Hassop Clo. Ches 4G 13
Hassop Clo. Dron 4G 3
Hassop Rd. Stav 6F 9
Hastings Clo. Ches 4H 13
Hathaway Clo. Old T 2D 34
Hathern Clo. Brim. 6H 15
Hatton Clo. Dron W 6B 2
Hatton Dri. Ches. 5F 13
Havens, The. Ches. 1H 21
Hawking Houses.
Ches 5H 13
Hawking La. Heath 6H 33
Hawkshead Av.
Dron W 5B 2
Hawksley Av. Ches. 5A 14
Hawthorn Clo. Clow. 4H 11
Hawthorne Av. Dron. 3E 3
Hawthorne Av.
Mas M 4A 10
Hawthorne Clo. Blbgh 2E 11
Hawthorne St. Ches. 3D 22
Hawthorn Hill. Stav 3F 9
Hawthorn Way. Ash. 5D 12
Haycroft Gdns.
Mas M 4A 10
Hayfield Clo. Dron W 5B 2
Hayfield Clo. Stav. 5F 9
Hayfield Clo. Wing. 3B 30
Hayford Way. Stav 1E 17
Hay La. Holy 6B 20
Hazel Clo. Dron 6G 3
Hazel Ct. Dron 6F 3
Hazel Dri. Ches 4H 21
Hazel Dri. Wing 3D 30
Hazel Gro. Mas M 4F 23
Hazelhurst. Has 6F 23
Hazelwood Clo.
Dron W 5A 2
Hazelwood Dri. Blbgh. 2F 11
Hazlehurst Av. Ches. 5C 14
Hazlehurst La. Ches. 5C 14
Headland Clo. Brim. 3G 15
Headland Rd. Brim 3G 15
Healaugh Way. Ches 4D 22
Heath. 4H 33
Heath Comn. Heath 3H 33
Heathcote Dri. Has 4G 23
Heath Ct. Ches. 4C 22
Heather Av. Heath. 4F 33
Heather Clo. Cal. 1A 24
Heather Gdns. Has 5G 23
Heather Va. Clo. Has 5G 23
Heather Va. Has. 5F 23
Heather Way. Holy 5B 20
Heathfield Av. Ches 1H 21
Heathfield Clo. Dron 6D 2
Heathfield Clo. Wing 2D 30
Heath Rd.
Hlmwd & Heath 6D 32
    (in two parts)
Heaton Clo. Dron W. 5B 2
Heaton St. Ches. 2G 21
Hedley Dri. Brim 2E 15
Helmsley Clo. Ches 3G 13
Helston Clo. Has 4D 22
Hemming Green. 6A 12
Henmoor. 4C 34
Henry St. Ches 2D 14
Henry St. Gras 3G 31
Hepthorne Lane. 1G 35
Hereford Dri. Brim. 2H 15
Heritage Dri. Clow 4H 11

Herriot Dri.—Lawrence Clo.

Herriot Dri. *Ches* 3D **22**
Hewers Holt. *Blbgh* 2F **11**
Heywood St. *Brim* 2G **15**
Heywood Vw. *Blbgh* 2G **11**
Hickinwood Cres. *Clow* 4G **19**
Hickinwood La. *Clow* 4G **19**
Hides Grn. *Bsvr* 2E **27**
Highashes La. *Asvr* 4C **28**
Highbury Rd. *Ches* 5B **14**
Higher Albert St. *Ches* 6C **14**
Highfield Av. *Ches* 5A **14**
Highfield La. *Ches* 4A **14**
Highfield Rd. *Bsvr* 3E **27**
Highfield Rd. *Ches* 5B **14**
Highfields. **6C** 32
Highfields Cres. *Dron* 6E **3**
Highfields Dri. *Hlmwd* 6D **32**
Highfields Rd. *Dron* 6E **3**
Highfields Way. *Hlmwd* 6D **32**
Highfield Ter. *Ches* 5B **14**
Highfield Vw. Rd. *Ches* 5B **14** (in two parts)
High Ga. Clo. *New W* 5F **7**
Highgate Dri. *Dron* 1G **5**
Highgate La. *Dron* 1F **5**
High Hazel Clo. *Clay C* 4G **35**
High Hazels Rd. *Blbgh* 3E **11**
High Hazel Wlk. Clay C 4G ***35*** *(off High Hazel Clo.)*
Highland Rd. *New W* 3F **7**
Highlands Pl. *Ches* 1B **14**
High La. *Walt* 1C **28**
Highleys Rd. *Clow* 6F **19**
Highlightly La. *Barl* 3A **4**
Highlow Clo. *Ches* 5G **13**
High St. *Blbgh* 1E **11**
High St. *Bsvr* 3E **27**
High St. *Brim* 2H **15**
High St. *Ches* 1C **22**
High St. *Clay C* 4E **35**
High St. *Clow* 6F **19**
High St. *Dron* 5E **3**
High St. *New W* 5E **7**
High St. *Old W* 6C **6**
High St. *Stav* 6E **9**
High Vw. Clo. *Ches* 2F **23**
High Wood Way *Blbgh* 3G **11**
Hillberry Ri. *Ches* 6B **22**
Hillcrest Gro. *Stav* 4F **9**
Hillcrest Rd. *Has* 5F **23**
Hill Gro. *Bar H* 4B **8**
Hillhouses La. *Wing* 3H **29**
Hillman Dri. *Ink* 4C **16**
Hillside Av. *Dron* 6E **3**
Hillside Dri. *Ches* 3H **21**
Hillside Dri. *Mas M* 5A **10**
Hillstown. **4G** 27
Hill St. *Clay C* 5E **35**
Hill Top. **6E** 3
Hill Top. *Bsvr* 1E **27**
Hilltop Rd. *Dron* 6E **3**
Hilltop Rd. *Old W* 6C **6**
Hilltop Rd. *Wing* 2H **29**
Hilltop Way. *Dron* 1F **5**
Hill Vw. Rd. *Brim* 2G **15**
Hillyfields. **6A** 32
Hipley Clo. *Ches* 4F **13**
Hipper St. *Ches* 2C **22**
Hipper St. S. *Ches* 2C **22**
Hipper St. W. *Ches* 2A **22**
Hoades St. *New T* 6E **31**
Hobner La. *Ink* 2C **16**
Hockley. **3C** 30
Hockley La. *Wing* 3C **30**
Hogarth Ri. *Dron* 6D **2**
Holbeach Dri. *Ches* 4A **22**
Holbeck Av. *Bsvr* 2G **27**
Holbeck Clo. *Ches* 6D **14**
Holbein Clo. *Dron* 6D **2**
Holborn Av. *Dron* 4E **3**
Holbrook Clo. *Ches* 4G **21**
Holbrook Pl. *Ink* 3C **16**
Holland Rd. *Old W* 6B **6**
Hollens Way. *Ches* 5D **12**
Hollies Clo. *Dron* 6G **3**
Hollin Clo. *Ches* 2G **13**
Hollingwood. **1A** 16
Hollingwood Cres. *Holl* 6A **8**
Hollingwood Est. *Holl* 1A **16**
Hollin Hill. *Clow* 5H **19**
Hollins Green. **5A** 34
Hollins Spring Av. *Dron* 6E **3**
Hollins Spring Rd. *Dron* 6E **3**
Hollis La. *Ches* 2D **22** (in two parts)
Hollythorpe Clo. *Has* 4F **23**
Holmbrook Wlk. *Ches* 5G **13**
Holm Clo. *Dron W* 4B **2**
Holmebank Clo. *Ches* 6A **14**
Holmebank E. *Ches* 6A **14**
Holmebank Vw. *Ches* 6A **14**
Holmebank W. *Ches* 6A **14**
Holme Brook Vw. *Ches* 4G **13**
Holme Hall Cres. *Ches* 4F **13**
Holme Pk. Av. *Ches* 3F **13**
Holme Rd. *Ches* 4C **14**
Holmesdale. **4G** 3
Holmesdale Clo. *Dron* 3G **3**
Holmesdale Rd. *Dron* 3F **3**
Holmesfield Rd. *Dron W* 5A **2**
Holme, The. *Dron* 3F **3**
Holmewood. **6E** 33
Holmewood Ind. Est. *Hlmwd* 6F **33**
Holmewood Ind. Pk. *Hlmwd* 4D **32**
Holmgate. **4A** 34
Holmgate Rd. *Clay C* 5A **34**
Holmley Bank. *Dron* 3E **3**
Holmley Common. **3E** 3
Holmley La. *Coal A* 3E **3**
Holymoor Rd. *Holy* 5B **20**
Holymoorside. **5B** 20
Holywell St. *Ches* 1C **22**
Homeport M. *Ches* 6C **14**
Hoodcroft La. *Stanf* 5E **11**
Hoole St. *Has* 4F **23**
Hope St. *Ches* 1A **22**
Hornbeam Clo. *Holl* 6A **8**
Hornscroft Rd. *Bsvr* 3E **27**
Horsehead La. *Bsvr* 2F **27**
Horsewood Rd. *Walt* 4F **21**
Horsley Clo. *Ches* 5E **13**
Houfton Cres. *Bsvr* 1D **26**
Houfton Rd. *Bsvr* 1D **26**
Houldsworth Cres. *Bsvr* 1D **26**
Houldsworth Dri. *Ches* 2F **23**
Howard Dri. *N Wing* 3H **35**
Howard Dri. *Old W* 6C **6**
Howden Clo. *Stav* 5F **9**
Howells Pl. *Mas M* 4H **9**
Hoylake Av. *Ches* 5G **21**
Hucklow Av. *Ches* 4B **22**
Hucklow Av. *Ink* 3C **16**
Hucklow Av. *N Wing* 6A **32**
Hucknall Av. *Ches* 6G **13**
Hudson Mt. *Bsvr* 4F **27**
Hundall. **1D** 6
Hundall La. *App* 1B **6**
Hundall La. *Ches* 4C **6**
Hungerhill La. *Holy* 2A **28**
Hunloke Av. *Ches* 3H **21**
Hunloke Cres. *Ches* 3A **22**
Hunloke Estate. **4E** 31
Hunloke Rd. *Hlmwd* 5E **33**
Hunloke Vw. *Wing* 2D **30**
Huntingdon Av. *Bsvr* 3F **27**
Huntley Clo. *Ink* 2B **16**
Huntsman Rd. *Stav* 6E **9**
Hutchings Cres. *Clow* 3H **11**
Hyndley Rd. *Bsvr* 2D **26**

I

Ians Way. *Ches* 6G **13**
Ilam Clo. *Ink* 4C **16**
Immingham Gro. *Stav* 1D **16**
Infirmary Rd. *Ches* 6D **14**
Ingleby Clo. *Dron W* 5A **2**
Ingleton Rd. *Has* 5D **22**
Ingmanthorpe. **3A** 12
Inkerman Cotts. *Ches* 6G **13**
Inkersall. **4D** 16
Inkersall Farm Cotts. *Stav* 4E **17**
Inkersall Green. **3C** 16
Inkersall Grn. Rd. *Ink* 2B **16**
Inkersall Rd. *Stav* 3E **17**
Intake Rd. *Bsvr* 2C **26**
Ireland Clo. *Stav* 6F **9**
Ireland Ind. Est. *Stav* 2E **17**
Ireland St. *Stav* 6F **9**
Iron Cliff Rd. *Bsvr* 1D **26**
Irongate. Ches 1C ***22*** *(off High St.)*
Ivanbrook Clo. *Dron W* 5A **2**
Ivanhoe Clo. *New T* 5F **31**
Ivy Clo. *Old W* 6C **6**
Ivy Spring Clo. *Wing* 2D **30**

J

Jackson Av. *New T* 6E **31**
Jackson Rd. *Dane* 5G **35**
Jago Av. *Clow* 5H **19**
James St. *Ches* 4C **14**
Jaw Bones Hill. *Ches* 4C **22**
Jebb Gdns. *Ches* 2G **21**
Jepson Rd. *Ches* 5E **23**
Jervis Pl. *Ink* 4B **16**
Johnstone Clo. *Ches* 3B **22**
John St. *Brim* 2G **15**
John St. *Ches* 1A **22**
John St. *Clay C* 4F **35**
John St. *Clow* 5H **11**
John St. *N Wing* 1G **35**
Jordanthorpe Parkway. *Shef* 1E **3**
Joseph Fletcher Dri. *Wing* 4B **30**
Jubilee Cotts. *Cal* 3A **24**
Jubilee Cres. *Clow* 5H **19**
Juniper Clo. *Holl* 6A **8**

K

Kariba Clo. *Ches* 1D **22**
Keats Rd. *Ches* 2B **14**
Keats Way. *Gras* 2G **31**
Kedleston Clo. *Ches* 3G **13**
Kedleston Ct. Stav 6E ***9*** *(off Devonshire St.)*
Keepers La. *Barl* 5C **4**
Keilder Ct. *Ches* 3H **21**
Kelburn Av. *Ches* 3G **21**
Kendal Dri. *Dron W* 5C **2**
Kendal Rd. *Ches* 2A **14**
Kenmere Clo. *Dane* 6F **35**
Kennet Va. *Ches* 5H **13**
Kenning St. *Clay C* 5E **35**
Kent Clo. *Ches* 5B **14**
Kentmere Clo. *Dron W* 5C **2**
Kent St. *Ches* 4E **23**
Kenwell Dri. *Shef* 1A **2**
Kenyon Rd. *Ches* 3G **23**
Kestrel Clo. *Bsvr* 1D **26**
Keswick Clo. *Bsvr* 3D **26**
Keswick Dri. *Ches* 3G **13** (in two parts)
Keswick Pl. *Dron W* 5B **2**
Kibworth Clo. *Ches* 5E **23**
Kidsley Clo. *Ches* 5E **13**
Kilburn Rd. *Dron W* 5A **2**
Kiln Hill. *Coal A* 3G **3**
Kinder Rd. *Ink* 4B **16**
Kingfisher Ct. *Bsvr* 1D **26**
Kingfisher Ho. *Old W* 5D **6**
Kingsclere Wlk. *Ches* 5B **22**
Kings Clo. *Clow* 6G **19**
Kingsley Av. *Ches* 4B **22**
Kingsmede Av. *Ches* 3H **21**
King St. *Brim* 1H **15**
King St. *Clay C* 5E **35**
King St. *Clow* 6F **19** (in two parts)
King St. N. *Ches* 3C **14**
King St. S. *Ches* 5C **22**
Kingswood Clo. *Ches* 2H **13**
Kipling Clo. *Dron* 1G **5**
Kipling Rd. *Ches* 2B **14**
Kirby Clo. *Ches* 5E **23**
Kirkdale Clo. *Ches* 4D **22**
Kirkstone Rd. *Ches* 2G **13**
Kitchen Wood La. *Dron W* 6A **2**
Knifesmith Ga. *Ches* 1C **22**
Knighton Clo. *Ches* 5D **22**
Knighton Ct. *N Wing* 2G **35**
Knighton St. *N Wing* 2G **35**
Knoll, The. *Ches* 2D **20**
Knoll, The. *Dron* 3H **3**

L

Laburnum Clo. *Bsvr* 3F **27**
Laburnum Ct. *Cal* 1A **24**
Laburnum St. *Holl* 1B **16**
Ladybower La. *Stav* 2D **16**
Ladywood Dri. *Ches* 3G **13**
Lakelands. *Wing* 4B **30**
Lakeside. *Wing* 4B **30**
Lakeside Clo. *Old W* 4E **7**
Lake Vw. Av. *Ches* 3G **21**
Lancaster Rd. *Ches* 2A **14**
Lancelot Clo. *Ches* 4H **21**
Landon Clo. *Walt* 5F **21**
Landseer Clo. *Dron* 6C **2**
Langdale Clo. *Ches* 5D **12**
Langdale Dri. *Dron* 3G **3**
Langdale Sq. *Brim* 2F **15**
Langer Fld. Av. *Ches* 5C **22**
Langer La. *Wing & Ches* 2A **30**
Langhurst Rd. *Ches* 6H **13**
Langley Clo. *Ches* 5E **13**
Langstone Av. *Bsvr* 3G **27**
Langtree Av. *Old W* 1C **14**
Langwith Rd. *Bsvr* 3E **27**
Lansbury Av. *Mas M* 5H **9**
Lansdowne Av. *Ches* 3A **14**
Lansdowne Rd. *Brim* 3F **15**
Larch Way. *Ches* 5H **13**
Lathkill Av. *Ink* 4C **16**
Lathkill Gro. *Dane* 6F **35**
Laurel Av. *Ark T* 2D **24**
Laurel Cres. *Holl* 1A **16**
Laurel Gth. Clo. *Old W* 5D **6**
Lawn, The. *Dron* 4F **3** (in two parts)
Lawn Vs. *Cal* 1A **24**
Lawrence Av. *Hlmwd* 5D **32**
Lawrence Clo. *Old W* 6C **6**

Laxfield Clo. *Ches* 4G **21**
Layton Dri. *Old W* 1D **14**
Leabrook Rd. *Dron W* 5A **2**
Leadhill Clo. *Ches* 6E **13**
Leander Ct. *Stav.* 6F **9**
Lea Rd. *Dron* 5E **3**
Lee Rd. *Ches.* 2G **23**
Lees Comn. *Barl* 3B **4**
Leeswood Clo. *Ches* 2H **13**
Leigh Way. *N Wing* 1H **35**
Lenthall's Bk. Row.
 Ches. 1H **21**
Levens Way. *Ches* 2A **14**
Leyburn Clo. *Ches* 5A **14**
Lichfield Rd. *Ches.* 4G **21**
Lilac Clo. *Heath* 4F **33**
Lilac Gro. *Bsvr.* 3G **27**
Lilac St. *Holl* 1A **16**
Lilleymede Clo. *Ches* 6B **22**
Lime Av. *Stav.* 1E **17**
Lime Clo. *Cal* 1A **24**
Limecroft Vw. *Wing* 3C **30**
Limekiln Field 1F **27**
Limekiln Fields Rd.
 Bsvr 2E **27**
Limekiln Way. *Blbgh* 2G **11**
Limetree Clo. *Brim* 4H **15**
Lime Tree Gro. *Ark T* 1D **24**
Lime Tree Gro. *Dane* 6G **35**
Linacre Av. *Dane* 6F **35**
Linacre Reservoirs Vis. Cen.
 . . . . 4B **12**
Linacre Rd. *Ches.* 6E **13**
Lincoln St. *Ches* 4C **22**
Lincoln Way. *N Wing* 2H **35**
Lindale Rd. *Ches* 1H **13**
Linden Av. *Ches* 3F **21**
Linden Av. *Clay C* 6F **35**
Linden Av. *Dron* 3F **3**
Linden Ct. *Clay C* 6F **35**
Linden Dri. *Has* 6F **23**
Linden Pk. Gro. *Ches.* 1A **22**
Lindisfarne Ct. *Ches* 3G **21**
Lindisfarne Rd. *Dron* 6F **3**
Lindrick Gdns. *Ches* 4G **21**
Lindrick Way. *Blbgh* 3F **11**
Lingfoot Av. *Shef* 1F **3**
Lingfoot Clo. *Shef* 1F **3**
Lingfoot Cres. *Shef* 1F **3**
Lingfoot Pl. *Shef* 1F **3**
Ling Rd. *Ches* 4H **21**
Lings Cres. *N Wing* 6A **32**
Links Rd. *Dron.* 6F **3**
Linnet Ho. *Old W* 5C **6**
Linscott Clo. *Ches* 3H **13**
Linton Rd. *Ches.* 4G **21**
Lit. Brind Rd. *Ches.* 3F **13**
Littlemoor. *Ches.* 3H **13**
Littlemoor Cen. *Ches.* 3A **14**
Littlemoor Cres. *Ches.* 3H **13**
Lit. Morton Rd.
 N Wing 2H **35**
Litton Clo. *Stav* 2C **16**
Loads Rd. *Holy* 5A **20**
Lockoford La. *Ches* 4C **14**
 (in four parts)
Lockoford Rd. *Ches.* 4C **14**
Loco Ter. *Has.* 6E **23**
Lodge Clo. *Brim.* 6A **16**
Lodge Dri. *Wing* 3C **30**
Lodge Farm Clo. *Walt.* 5F **21**
Lodge Pl. *Ink* 4C **16**
Lodge Wlk. *Ink* 4C **16**
London St. *New W* 5F **7**
Longacre Rd. *Dron* 1E **5**
Longcliff Wlk. *Ches* 4H **13**
Longcourse La. *Duck* 2G **25**
Longcroft Av. *Dron W* 4A **2**
Longcroft Clo. *New T* 6F **31**
Longcroft Ct. *Ches.* 5B **22**
Longcroft Cres.
 Dron W 4A **2**
Longcroft Rd. *Dron W* 4A **2**

Long Duckmanton 1G **25**
Longedge Gro. *Wing* 2C **30**
Longedge La. *Wing* 3A **30**
Longedge Ri. *Wing* 3D **30**
Longfield Grange.
 Ches 4G **13**
Longlands. *Bsvr.* 2F **27**
Long La. *Kil* 1E **7**
Long Shambles. *Ches* 1C **22**
 (off High St.)
Longshaw Clo.
 N Wing 2H **35**
Longshaw Clo. *Stav.* 2D **16**
Lord Roberts Rd. *Ches* . . . 3C **22**
Lords Clo. *Bsvr* 3E **27**
Lordsmill Ga. *Ches* 2D **22**
Lordsmill St. *Ches.* 2D **22**
Lorne Clo. *Dron W* 4B **2**
Loundes Rd. *Uns.* 2A **6**
Loundes Wood Av.
 Ches 2G **13**
Loundsley Green. 5G **13**
Loundsley Grn. Rd.
 Ches 6F **13**
Low Comn. *Ren.* 1B **10**
Lowedges. 1D **2**
Low Edges. *Shef* 1E **3**
Lowedges Cres. *Shef.* 1D **2**
Lowedges Dri. *Shef.* 1D **2**
Lowedges Pl. *Shef.* 1E **3**
Lowedges Rd. *Shef* 1B **2**
Lower All. *Cal.* 3A **24**
Lower Bradway. 1A **2**
Lwr. Grove Rd. *Ches* 1B **22**
Lwr. Mantle Clo.
 Clay C 4F **35**
Lowfields. *Stav.* 6G **9**
Lowgates. *Stav.* 6F **9**
Low Pavement. *Ches.* 1C **22**
Low Rd. *Stanf* 1E **19**
Lowry Dri. *Dron.* 5D **2**
Loxley Clo. *Ches* 1F **21**
Lucas Rd. *Ches* 4A **14**
Ludham Clo. *Ches* 3B **14**
Ludham Gdns. *Ches* 3B **14**
Lumsdale Rd. *Stav* 2C **16**
Lundy Rd. *Dron* 6F **3**
Lupin Way. *Cal.* 1A **24**
Lydden Clo. *Brim.* 2G **15**
Lydford Av. *Old W* 1D **14**
Lydgate Dri. *Wing* 3A **30**
Lynham Clo. *Dane.* 5G **35**
Lynwood Clo. *Dron W* 5B **2**

M

M1 Commerce Pk.
 Duck 5H **17**
Macdonald Clo. *Gras* 3H **31**
Machin Ct. *Dron.* 4E **3**
McMahon Av. *Ink* 4B **16**
MacMillan M. *Ches* 1F **21**
Madin Dri. *Ink* 4B **16**
Madin St. *Ches* 6C **14**
Madin St. *New T* 6F **31**
Main Rd. *App.* 1A **6**
Main Rd. *Barl.* 6C **4**
Main Rd. *Cut* 3C **12**
Main Rd. *Heath.* 4H **33**
Main Rd. *Mar L* 4F **7**
Main St. *Ches* 4D **26**
Main St. *Pal.* 6E **27**
Main St. *Scar.* 6H **27**
Malham Clo. *Ches.* 5H **13**
Malia Rd. *Ches.* 4E **15**
Malkin St. *Ches.* 1D **22**
Mallard Ct. *Stav.* 6F **9**
Mallory Clo. *Ches.* 5A **14**
Malson Way. *Ches.* 4B **14**
Malthouse Ct. *Ches.* 6C **14**

Malthouse La. *Wing.* 3F **29**
Malton Wlk. *Ches* 5B **22**
Malvern Rd. *Ches* 6A **14**
Manifold Av. *Stav.* 2D **16**
Manknell Rd. *Ches.* 2C **14**
Manor Av. *Brim.* 3H **15**
Manor Bungalows.
 Dron. 5D **2**
Manor Ct. *Clow* 6G **19**
Mnr. Court Rd. *Bsvr* 1D **26**
Manor Cres. *Ches* 1H **21**
Manor Cres. *Dron* 5D **2**
Manor Dri. *Brim* 3H **15**
Manor Dri. *Ches* 1G **21**
 (in two parts)
Mnr. Farm M. *Duck* 1G **25**
Manor Gro. *Blbgh* 2E **11**
Manor Rd. *Blbgh* 1E **11**
Manor Rd. *Brim.* 3H **15**
Manor Rd. *Ches* 1G **21**
 (in two parts)
Mansfeldt Cres. *Ches.* 4A **14**
Mansfeldt Rd. *Ches.* 4A **14**
Mansfield Rd.
 Ches & Temp N. 5F **23**
Mansfield Rd.
 Clow . . . . 6F **19** & 2H **19**
Mansfield Rd. *Pal.* 6F **27**
Mansfield Rd. *Scar* 6H **27**
Manvers Rd. *Cal* 6A **16**
Maple Ter. *Holl.* 2B **16**
Mapperley Rd. *Dron W* . . . 5A **2**
Marchwood Clo. *Ches* 6B **14**
Mardale Clo. *Ches* 1A **14**
Marine Dri. *Ches* 1E **23**
Market Hall. *Ches* 1C **22**
Market Pl. *Bsvr* 3E **27**
Market Pl. *Ches.* 1C **22**
Market Pl. *Stav.* 6E **9**
Market St. *Clay C* 5E **35**
Market St. *Stav.* 6E **9**
Markham Ct. *Duck.* 5G **17**
 (Duckmanton Rd.)
Markham Ct. *Duck.* 5H **17**
 (Markham Rd.)
Markham Cres. *Stav.* 6F **9**
Markham La. *Duck.* 6H **17**
Markham Quay.
 Ches 2D **22**
 (off Camlough Wlk.)
Markham Ri. *Clay C.* 4D **34**
Markham Rd. *Ches* 2B **22**
Markham Rd. *Duck.* 5G **17**
Markham Vs. *Duck.* 5G **17**
 (off Markham Rd.)
Markland Av. *Clow.* 5H **19**
Markland Cres. *Clow.* 5H **19**
Markland La. *Clow.* 6H **19**
Marlborough Links Golf
 Course. 3F **11**
Marlpit La. *Bsvr.* 2F **27**
Marsden Pl. *Ches* 2H **21**
 (Chatsworth Rd.)
Marsden Pl. *Ches* 6C **14**
 (Spencer St.)
Marsden St. *Ches* 1C **22**
Marsh Av. *Dron* 3F **3**
Marshfield Gro. *Stav.* 6G **9**
Marston Clo. *Dron W* 6B **2**
Martins La. *Old T.* 6C **30**
Marx Ct. *Clay C* 5E **35**
Mary Ann St. *Ches.* 4A **6**
Masefield Av. *Hlmwd.* 6D **32**
Masson Clo. *Ches* 5H **13**
Mastin Av. *Clow.* 3H **11**
Mastin Moor. 4A **10**
Mather's Way. *New T.* 5F **31**
Matlock Dri. *Ink.* 5C **16**
Matlock Rd.
 Asvr, Walt & Ches. 4C **28**
May Av. *Old W* 5E **7**
Mayfield Dri. *N Wing* 2H **35**
Mayfield Rd. *Ches.* 2G **21**

Maynard Rd. *Ches* 3B **22**
Meadow Clo. *Blbgh* 2G **11**
Meadow Clo. *Ches* 4E **27**
Meadow Clo. *Coal A* 2G **3**
Meadow Clo. *New W* 6F **7**
Meadow Ct. *New W* 4F **7**
 (off Handley Rd.)
Meadow Cft. *Hlmwd* 6D **32**
Meadowhill Rd. *Has.* 4F **23**
Meadowlands. *Bsvr.* 2G **27**
Meadow Ri. *Ash* 6D **12**
Meadow Rd. *Clay C* 4C **34**
Meadows Dri. *Stav.* 1E **17**
Meadowside Clo.
 Wing 2C **30**
Meadows, The. *Ash* 5D **12**
Meadow Vw. *Ches* 4E **21**
Meadow Vw. *Clow.* 6G **19**
Meadow Vw. *Hlmwd* 6C **32**
Mead, The. *Has* 4E **23**
Meakin St. *Has.* 4F **23**
Medlock Clo. *Walt.* 5F **21**
Medlock Rd. *Ches.* 4G **21**
Melbourne Av. *Dron W* . . . 5A **2**
Melbourne Ct. *Stav* 6E **9**
 (off Devonshire St.)
Melling Clo. *Ches.* 4B **22**
Melling Ct. *Ches* 4B **22**
Mellor La. *Barl.* 1C **12**
Mellor Way. *Ches.* 5C **22**
Melrose Clo. *Ches.* 1G **21**
Meltham La. *Ches* 4D **14**
Melville Cres. *Brim* 6H **15**
Mendip Cres. *Ches.* 6F **13**
Mercaston Clo. *Ches* 5E **13**
Merlin Av. *Bsvr* 1D **26**
Merrick Clo. *Ches* 5H **13**
Meynell Clo. *Ches* 6F **13**
Michael Clo. *Wing* 1C **30**
Mickley. 3A **2**
Middlecroft. 2C **16**
Middlecroft Rd. *Stav* 3C **16**
Middle La. *Dane* 5G **35**
Middle Pavement. *Ches*
 (off Low Pavement)
 . . . . 1C **22**
Middle Rd. *Wing* 5A **30**
Middle Shambles.
 Ches 1C **22**
 (off Shambles, The)
Middle Shambles.
 Ches 1C **22**
 (off High St.)
Middle St. *Bsvr* 4G **27**
Middleton Dri. *Ink* 5B **16**
Middletown Meadows.
 Blbgh 2E **11**
Midland Ct. *Has.* 5D **22**
Midland Ter. *Bar H.* 4B **8**
Midland Ter. *Has* 5D **22**
 (in two parts)
Midland Vw. *N Wing* 1H **35**
Midland Way. *Blbgh* 3E **11**
Midway Cen. *Clay C* 4F **35**
Milehill. 1H **31**
Milford Rd. *Ink* 5C **16**
Milking La. *Clow* 5F **11**
Mill Clo. *Clow.* 5F **19**
Mill Cotts. *Old T.* 3A **34**
Mill Cres. *Wing* 3E **31**
Millcross La. *Barl.* 5C **4**
Milldale Clo. *Ches* 5G **13**
Millennium Way.
 Ches 1A **14**
Miller Av. *Mas M* 4A **10**
Millfield Pk. (Cvn. Site)
 Old T. 3B **34**
Mill Grn. *Stav.* 6E **9**
Mill Hill. *Sut S.* 6H **25**
Mill Ho. M. *Stav.* 6E **9**
Mill La. *Bsvr.* 1E **27**
Mill La. *Ches* 2H **21**
Mill La. *Dron* 5F **3**

Mill La. *Heath* 4H **33**
    (in two parts)
Mill La. *Old T.* 3A **34**
Mill La. *Stanf.* 2C **18**
Mill La. *Wing* 3E **31**
    (in three parts)
Millstone Clo. *Dron W.* 4B **2**
Mill Stream Clo. *Ches* . . . 3G **21**
Mill St. *Barl* 5B **4**
Mill St. *Ches* 1D **22**
Mill St. *Clow.* 5F **19**
Mill Wlk. *Bsvr* 1E **27**
Milton Cres. *Ches* 4C **22**
Milton Pl. *Stav* 6F **9**
Minimum Ter. *Ches* 2A **22**
Miriam Av. *Ches.* 4E **21**
Mitchell St. *Clow* 5G **19**
Mitchell Way. *New W.* 5G **7**
Mods La. *Barl* 5B **4**
Molineux Av. *Stav* 1D **16**
Monkwood Rd. *Ches* 2H **13**
Monnies End. *Clow* 3G **11**
Monsal Cres. *Ink* 4B **16**
Montrose Pl. *Dron W.* 4B **2**
Monyash Clo. *Stav.* 3C **16**
Moonpenny Way. *Dron* . . . 5E **3**
Mooracre La. *Bsvr.* 3G **27**
Moore Clo. *Hlmwd* 5D **32**
Moorfield Av. *Bsvr* 3F **27**
Moorfield Sq. *Bsvr.* 3F **27**
Moorgate Cres. *Dron* 6F **3**
Moorhay Clo. *Ches.* 3F **13**
Moorland Dri. *Heath.* 4F **33**
Moorland Vw. Rd. *Ches.* . . 4G **21**
Moor La. *Bsvr* 3F **27**
Moor La. *Cal* 5C **24**
Moorlawn Av. *Holy.* 5C **20**
Moor Pk. Av. *Ches.* 4G **21**
Moorview Clo. *Brim.* 3F **15**
Moorview Clo. *Wing* 3D **30**
Moor Vw. Rd. *Stav* 6G **9**
Moray Pl. *Dron W.* 4B **2**
Morley Av. *Ches.* 6G **13**
Morley Clo. *Dron W.* 5A **2**
Mornington Rd. *Hlmwd.* . . 6D **32**
Morris Av. *Ches.* 5A **14**
Morris Dri. *Ches* 5A **14**
Morton Av. *Clay C* 4D **34**
Morven Av. *Bsvr.* 3F **27**
Moston Wlk. *Ches.* 5A **22**
Mound Rd. *Ches* 3C **22**
Mountcastle St. *Ches.* . . . 2B **14**
Mountcastle Wlk. *Ches* . . 2B **14**
Mount Pleasant. *Old W* . . 5C **6**
Muirfield Clo. *Ches* 4D **14**
Mulberry Clo. *Wing* 2C **30**
Musard Pl. *Stav.* 1D **16**
Myrtle Gro. *Holl* 1A **16**

N

Nairn Dri. *Dron W* 5B **2**
Neale Bank. *Brim* 3F **15**
Neale St. *Clow.* 5G **19**
Nelson St. *Ches.* 4C **14**
Nesbit St. *Bsvr.* 4F **27**
Nesfield. 1D **12**
Nesfield Clo. *Ches.* 2H **13**
Nether Chanderhill. 3A **20**
Nether Clo. *Wing* 4C **30**
Nether Cft. Clo. *Brim* 3G **15**
Nethercroft La. *Dane* 5G **35**
Netherdene Rd. *Dron* 5E **3**
    (in two parts)
Nether Farm Clo. *Brim.* . . . 5H **15**
Netherfield Clo. *Stav* 6G **9**
Netherfield Rd. *Ches* 4E **21**
Netherfields Cres.
    Dron 6E **3**
Nether Handley. 1H **7**

Netherleigh Ct. *Ches* 1F **21**
Netherleigh Rd. *Ches* 1F **21**
Nether Moor. 5C **30**
Nethermoor Rd.
    Old T. 1E **35**
Nethermoor Rd.
    Wing. 4B **30**
Nether Springs Rd.
    Bsvr 1D **26**
Netherthorpe. 6F **9**
Netherthorpe. *Stav.* 6G **9**
Netherthorpe Clo. *Stav.* . . 6F **9**
Netherthorpe Rd. *Stav.* . . . 6F **9**
Nevis Clo. *Ches* 6H **13**
New Barlborough. 3H **11**
New Barlborough Clo.
    Clow 3H **11**
New Beetwell St.
    Ches. 1C **22**
Newbold. 4H **13**
Newbold Av. *Ches* 4A **14**
Newbold Bk. La. *Ches.* . . 4H **13**
    (in two parts)
Newbold Ct. *Ches* 3H **13**
Newbold Dri. *Ches.* 4A **14**
Newbold Moor. 2B **14**
Newbold Rd. *Ches* 2E **13**
Newbold Village. 4A **14**
New Bolsover. 3C **26**
New Bolsover. *Bsvr* 3C **26**
Newbridge Ct. *Old W.* . . . 1C **14**
Newbridge Dri. *Brim* 2F **15**
Newbridge La.
    Old W & Brim. 6C **6**
    (in three parts)
Newbridge St. *Old W.* . . . 1C **14**
New Brimington. 1H **15**
Newby Rd. *Ches* 2G **13**
Newgate. 1B **12**
New Hall Rd. *Ches.* 2H **21**
New Haven Clo. *Ches.* . . 3F **21**
New Houses. *Ches.* 1E **23**
Newland Dale. *Ches.* . . . 6C **14**
Newland Gdns. *Ches.* . . . 5A **14**
Newlands Av. *Ches* 1G **21**
Newmarket. 5C **34**
New market La. *Clay C* . . 5A **34**
New Queen St. *Ches* 6C **14**
New Rd. *Blbgh.* 1F **11**
New Rd. *Holy.* 5B **20**
New Rd. *Wing* 3A **30**
New Sq. *Ches* 1C **22**
New Sta. Rd. *Bsvr.* 3D **26**
Newstead Clo. *Dron W* . . 5A **2**
New St. *Bsvr* 1E **27**
New St. *Ches* 2C **22**
New St. *Gras.* 3G **31**
New St. *N Wing.* 2G **35**
Newtons Cft. Cres.
    Blbgh. 2F **11**
New Whittington. 5F **7**
Nicholas St. *Has.* 5F **23**
Nightingale Clo. *Dane* . . 6G **35**
Nook La. *Cal* 1B **24**
Norbriggs. 5H **9**
Norbriggs Rd. *Mas M* . . . 5H **9**
Norbury Clo. *Ches* 5F **13**
Norbury Clo. *Dron W.* . . . 5B **2**
Norfolk Av. *Gras* 4H **31**
Norfolk Clo. *Walt* 4F **21**
North Clo. *Uns* 2A **6**
North Cres. *Duck.* 4G **17**
Northern Comn.
    Dron W 3A **2**
Northfield La. *Pal.* 6F **27**
Northfields. *Clow.* 6G **19**
North Gro. *Duck.* 4G **17**
North La. *Old Br* 6B **12**
N. Moor Clo. *Brim.* 3H **15**
Northmoor Vw. *Brim.* . . . 3H **15**
North Rd. *Cal.* 1H **23**
North Rd. *Clow* 5F **19**
North Side. *New T.* 5E **31**

North St. *Clay C.* 3C **34**
North St. *N Wing.* 2G **35**
North Ter. *Has.* 5D **22**
N. View St. *Bsvr.* 4C **26**
North Wingfield. 1H **35**
N. Wingfield Rd. *Gras* . . 1F **31**
Norton Av. *Ches.* 4E **21**
Norton Av. *Shut.* 4D **18**
Norwood Av. *Has.* 5F **23**
Norwood Clo. *Has.* 6G **23**
Nottingham Clo.
    Wing. 3D **30**
Nottingham Dri.
    Wing. 3D **30**
Nursery Dri. *Bsvr.* 2D **26**
Nuttack La. *Old Br* 6B **12**
    (in two parts)

O

Oadby Dri. *Ches.* 5E **23**
Oakamoor Clo. *Ches.* . . . 5F **13**
Oak Bank Av. *Old W.* . . . 5D **6**
Oak Clo. *Brim.* 3F **15**
Oak Cres. *Wing* 3B **30**
Oakdale Clo. *Dane* 6G **35**
Oakdell. *Dron.* 3H **3**
Oakfield Av. *Ches.* 3F **21**
Oakhill Rd. *Dron* 4G **3**
Oaklea Way. *Old T.* 2D **34**
Oakley Av. *Ches.* 6A **14**
Oak Rd. *Gras.* 3H **31**
Oaks Farm La. *Cal.* 2A **24**
Oaks La. *Barl* 1A **12**
Oak St. *Holl* 1A **16**
Oak Tree Clo. *Ark T.* . . . 1D **24**
Oak Tree Cotts. *Cal* 3A **24**
Oak Tree Rd. *Clow* 6F **19**
Oakwood Way. *Mas M.* . . 4H **9**
Occupation Clo. *Blbgh* . . 2E **11**
Occupation La. *N Wing* . . 2G **35**
Occupation Rd. *Ches* . . . 2B **14**
Offridge Clo. *Clow* 6G **19**
Old Bakery Clo. *Old W.* . . 6C **6**
Old Brampton. 6B **12**
Old Brick Works La.
    Ches 4C **14**
Old Colliery La. *Hlmwd* . . 6E **33**
Old Hall Rd. *Ches* 2H **21**
Old Hill. *Bsvr* 2E **27**
Old Ho. Rd. *Ches.* 4H **13**
Old Houses. *Ches* 1E **23**
Old Mill Dri. *Ches.* 3E **13**
Old Peverel Rd. *Duck.* . . 5G **17**
Old Quarry Clo. *Blbgh* . . 2F **11**
Oldridge Clo. *Ches.* 4F **13**
Old Rd. *Ches* 1E **21**
Old School La. *Cal.* 2H **23**
Old Sta. Yd. *Brim.* 2E **15**
Old Tupton. 1E **35**
Old Whittington. 6C **6**
Old Whittington La. *Uns* . . 2A **6**
Orchard Clo. Blbgh. 1E **11**
    (off West End)
Orchard Clo. *Bsvr.* 3F **27**
Orchard Clo. *Clow* 6F **19**
Orchard Sq. *Dron W* 4B **2**
Orchards Way. *Ches* 3G **21**
Orchard Vw. *Bsvr* 4D **26**
Orchard Vw. Rd. *Ches* . . 6G **13**
Orchid Clo. *Cal.* 1A **24**
Ormesby Clo. *Dron W.* . . 5A **2**
Ormond Clo. *Walt.* 5F **21**
Ormsby Rd. *Ches* 3B **14**
Orwins Clo. *Ches.* 3H **13**
Outram Rd. *Ches.* 4B **14**
Ovencroft La. *Bsvr.* 1G **27**
Overlees. *Barl* 5B **4**
Overton Clo. *Stav.* 5F **9**
Over Woodhouse. 1D **26**
Owen Falls Av. *Ches.* . . . 1E **23**

Owlcotes Vw. *Bsvr.* 4E **27**
Owler Car La. *Coal A.* . . . 2H **3**
Ox Clo. *Clay C* 4F **35**
Oxclose Dri. *Dron W.* . . . 5A **2**
Oxclose La. *Dron W.* . . . 5A **2**
Oxcroft. 2G **19**
Oxcroft Estate. 3G **19**
Oxcroft La.
    Bsvr . . . . . . 2E **27** & 3G **19**
Oxcroft Way. *Blbgh* 2F **11**
Oxford Clo. *Brim* 2H **15**
Oxford Rd. *Brim* 2H **15**
Oxton Rakes. 2A **12**

P

Packer's Row. *Ches* 1C **22**
Paddock Clo. *Wing* 3C **30**
Paddocks, The. *Mas M* . . 5A **10**
Paddock, The. *Bsvr* 3F **27**
Paddock Way. *Dron* 3F **3**
    (Holmesdale Rd.)
Paddock Way. *Dron* 4F **3**
    (Stonelow Rd.)
Padley Way. *N Wing* . . . 3H **35**
Paisley Clo. *Stav* 2C **16**
Palmer Cres. *Dron* 5F **3**
Palmersgate. *Ches.* 1C **22**
    (off Parker's Row)
Palterton. 6E **27**
Palterton La. *Sut S* 6G **25**
    (in two parts)
Pankhurst Pl. *Clay C* . . . 5E **35**
Park Av. *Dron.* 4F **3**
Park Clo. *Ches.* 5C **22**
Park Dri. *Ches.* 3D **22**
Parker Av. *Cal* 6H **15**
Parkers Yd. *Ches.* 1D **22**
Park Farm. *Dron W* 4A **2**
Parkfields. *Clow.* 6F **19**
Parkgate La.
    Mar L & New W. 3G **7**
Park Hall Av. *Walt.* 4E **21**
Park Hall Rd. *Walt.* 5F **21**
Park Hall Gdns. *Walt.* . . 4F **21**
Parkhouse Clo. *Clay C.* . . 4D **34**
Parkhouse Rd. *Lwr P* . . . 3H **35**
Parkland Dri. *Wing* 4C **30**
Park La. *Ches* 3B **14**
Park Rd. *Ches* 3B **22**
Park Rd. *Hlmwd* 5D **32**
Park Rd. *Old T.* 1E **35**
Park Row. *Clay C* 4F **35**
Parkside. *Ches.* 3C **14**
Parkside Vw. *Ches* 4E **13**
Park St. *Blbgh* 1F **11**
Park St. *Ches.* 5C **22**
Park Vw. *Blbgh.* 1F **11**
Park Vw. *Clow.* 4G **19**
Park Vw. *Has.* 5F **23**
Park Vw. *N Wing.* 1H **35**
Parwich Clo. *Ches* 5E **13**
Parwich Rd. *N Wing* 2H **35**
Paton Gro. *Brim.* 2F **15**
Patterdale Clo. *Dron W* . . 5C **2**
Pattison St. *Shut.* 4D **18**
Pavilion Clo. *Ink.* 3C **16**
Pavilion Workshops.
    Hlmwd 5D **32**
Paxton Rd. *Ches* 5E **15**
Peacock Heritage Cen.
    . . . . 1C **22**
Peakley Hill. 3A **4**
Peak Pl. *Ink.* 3D **16**
Peak Vw. *Clow.* 3H **11**
Peak Vw. Rd. *Ches.* 6H **13**
Pearce La. *Wing* 3G **29**
Pearson Cft. *Ches.* 4G **13**
Peartree Av. *Wing* 3A **30**
Pear Tree Clo. *Holl* 2A **16**
Peel Gdns. *Dron* 5D **2**

Pegasus Ct. *Bsvr* 3F **27**
Peggars Clo. *Blbgh* 2F **11**
Pembroke Clo. *Ches* 3G **21**
Pembroke Ct. *Ches* 3A **14**
Pembroke Rd. *Dron* 6E **3**
Penistone Gdns. *Dane* 6F **35**
Penmore Clo. *Has* 3E **23**
Penmore Gdns. *Has.* 4E **23**
Penmore La. *Has* 4E **23**
Penmore St. *Has* 4E **23**
Penncroft Dri. *Dane* 5F **35**
Penncroft La. *Dane* 6F **35**
Pennine Vw. *Pal.* 6E **27**
Pennine Wlk. Gras. 3H **31**
. . . . (off Pennine Way)
Pennine Way. *Ches* 5G **13**
Pennine Way. *Gras* 3H **31**
Pennywell Dri. *Holy* 5B **20**
Penrose Cres. *Ark T* 1D **24**
Pentland Clo. *Ches* 5G **13**
Pentland Rd. *Dron W* 5B **2**
Peterdale Clo. *Brim* 2G **15**
Peterdale Rd. *Brim* 2G **15**
Peters Av. *Clay C* 4D **34**
Pettyclose La. *Ches* 5F **15**
Pevensey Av. *Ches.* 4A **14**
Pevensey Ct. *Ches* 3A **14**
Peveril Rd. *Bsvr.* 1D **26**
Peveril Rd. *Ches* 3B **14**
Pewit Clo. *Hlmwd* 6D **32**
Piccadilly Rd. *Ches* 2D **22**
Pickman Cotts. *New T* 6F **31**
Pickton Clo. *Ches* 2H **21**
Pighills La. *Coal A* 2F **3**
Pike Clo. *Ches* 5F **13**
Pilsley Rd. *Dane* 5G **35**
Pindale Av. *Ink.* 3C **16**
Pine St. *Holl.* 2A **16**
Pine Vw. *Ches* 1F **21**
Pine Vw. *Dane* 6G **35**
Pinfold Clo. *Holy* 4C **20**
Pingle Grange. *Brim* 3G **15**
Piper Av. *Clay C* 4G **35**
Piper La. *Old Br* 1C **20**
Pitch Clo. *Clow* 6H **11**
Pit La. *Dane* 5G **35**
Plantation Clo. *Ches.* 5E **13**
Pleasant Av. *Bsvr* 5F **27**
Pleasant Pl. *Ches.* 1H **21**
Plover Way. *Cal* 1H **23**
Pocknedge La. *Holy* 3B **20**
Polyfields La. *Bsvr* 4F **27**
Pond La. *New T* 6F **31**
Pond La. *Wing.* 2A **30**
Pond St. *Ches* 2C **22**
Pondwell Dri. *Brim* 3H **15**
Poolsbrook. 2G **17**
Poolsbrook Av. *Pool* 2G **17**
Poolsbrook Country Pk.
. . . . 3E **17**
Poolsbrook Cres. *Pool.* . . . 2G **17**
Poolsbrook Rd. *Duck* 4G **17**
Poolsbrook Sq. *Pool* 2G **17**
Poolsbrook Vw. *Pool* 2G **17**
Pool's La. *Mar L* 1E **7**
Poplar Av. *Ches* 2F **21**
Poplar Clo. *Dron* 1G **5**
Poplar Dri. *New T* 5E **31**
Poplar Pl. *Ches* 2B **14**
Poplars, The. Gras. 3G **31**
. . . . (off Mill La.)
Porter St. *Stav* 6E **9**
Portland Av. *Bsvr* 3F **27**
Portland Cres. *Bsvr* 3F **27**
Portland St. *Clow* 5H **19**
Postmans La. *Temp N* 2C **32**
Potters Clo. *Old W.* 6D **6**
Pottery La. E. *Ches* 3D **14**
Pottery La. W. *Ches* 3C **14**
Pratthall. 3A **12**
Press La.
Old T . . . . . . 6G **29** & 2A **34**
Prestwold Way. *Ches* 5E **23**

Pretoria St. *Shut* 4D **18**
Priestfield Gdns. *Ches* . . . 3F **13**
Princess Pl. *Clay C* 6E **35**
Princess Rd. *Dron* 4E **3**
Princess St. *Brim* 1H **15**
Princess St. *Ches* 6B **14**
Pringle La. *Ches* 4B **6**
Priory Clo. *Walt* 5F **21**
Private Dri. *Holl* 2A **16**
Prospect Rd. *Dron.* 3G **3**
Prospect Rd. *Old W.* 6B **6**
Prospect Ter. *Ches* 6A **14**
Pullman Clo. *Stav.* 5F **9**
Purbeck Av. *Ches.* 6H **13**
Pynot Rd. *Old W* 6D **6**

Q

Quantock Way. *Ches* 5F **13**
Quarry Bank Rd. *Ches* . . . 2E **23**
Quarry La. *Ches.* 2G **21**
Quarry Rd. *Bsvr.* 1E **27**
Queen Mary Rd. *Ches* . . . 3F **21**
Queen St. *Brim* 1H **15**
Queen St. *Ches* 6B **14**
Queen St. *Clay C* 6E **35**
Queen St. *Stav.* 2D **16**
Queen St. N. *Ches* 2C **14**
Queens Wlk. *Hlmwd* 5E **33**
Queen's Wlk. New T 5F **31**
. . . . (off Mather's Way)
Queensway. *Hlmwd* 5E **33**
Queen's Way. *New T* 5F **31**
Queen Victoria Rd.
New T 5E **31**
Quoit Green. 5F **3**
Quoit Grn. *Dron* 5F **3**
Quorn Dri. *Ches.* 5E **13**

R

Racecourse Mt. *Ches.* 2B **14**
Racecourse Rd. *Ches* 2B **14**
Radbourne Comn.
Dron W 5B **2**
Railway Cotts. *Cor.* 1H **31**
Railway Cotts. *Hlmwd* . . 5F **33**
Railway Ter. *Has* 5D **22**
Ralph Rd. *Stav* 6G **9**
Ramper Av. *Ches* 6H **11**
Ramsey Av. *Ches.* 3H **21**
Ramshaw Clo. *Ches* 3G **13**
Ramshaw Rd. *Uns.* 2A **6**
Raneld Mt. *Ches* 4G **21**
Ranmoor Clo. *Has.* 4E **23**
Ratcliffe Clo. *Ches.* 5E **23**
Ravensdale Clo. *Ink.* 5C **16**
Ravensdale Rd.
Dron W 5A **2**
Ravenside Retail Pk.
Ches 2C **22**
Ravenswood Rd.
Ches 5E **13**
Rawlins Ct. *Coal A.* 2G **3**
Rayleigh Av. *Brim.* 2F **15**
Recreation Clo. *Clow* 5F **19**
Recreation Rd. *Brim* 5H **15**
Rectory Clo. *Duck* 1G **25**
Rectory Dri. *Wing* 2A **30**
Rectory Rd. *Clow.* 5F **19**
Rectory Rd. *Duck* 1G **25**
Rectory Rd. *Stav* 6E **9**
Redacre Rd. *Bsvr* 3G **27**
Redbrook Av. *Has* 4D **22**
Redfern St. *New T* 1E **35**
Redgrove Way. *Ches* 4G **21**
Red Ho. Clo. *New W* 4F **7**
Red Ho. Wlk. *Ches* 5H **13**
Red La. *Old W* 1E **15**

Rednall Clo. *Ches.* 5E **13**
Redvers Buller Rd.
Ches 3C **22**
Redwood Clo. *Holl.* 2A **16**
Regent St. *Clow.* 4H **11**
Rembrandt Dri. *Dron.* 5C **2**
Rempstone Dri. *Ches* 5D **22**
Renishaw. 1H **9**
Renishaw Rd. *Mas M* 3A **10**
Repton Clo. *Ches.* 5E **13**
Repton Pl. *Dron W* 5A **2**
Reservoir Ter. *Ches* 6A **14**
Revolution House. 5C **6**
Reynolds Clo. *Dron* 6C **2**
Rhodes Av. *Ches* 5A **14**
Rhodes Cotts. *Clow* 5G **19**
Rhodesia Rd. *Ches* 2G **21**
Riber Clo. *Ink.* 5C **16**
Riber Cres. *Old T.* 3D **34**
Riber Ter. *Ches* 2A **22**
Richmond Clo. *Ches* 4A **22**
Riddings Cft. *Ches.* 4G **13**
Ridd Way. *Wing.* 3C **30**
Ridgedale Rd. *Bsvr* 3E **27**
Ridgeway. *Dron* 3H **3**
Ridgeway Av. *Bsvr.* 2G **27**
Ridgway. *Clow.* 6G **19**
Riggotts La. *Walt.* 5H **21**
Riggotts Way. *Cut* 2C **12**
Ringer La. *Clow* 6F **19**
Ringer Way. *Clow.* 6F **19**
Ringwood Av. *Ches* 3A **14**
Ringwood Av. *Stav.* 2C **16**
Ringwood Rd. *Brim.* 2H **15**
Ringwood Vw. *Brim.* 3H **15**
Riverdale Pk. Cvn. Site.
Stav 5G **9**
Riverside Cres. *Holy* 5C **20**
Riverside Way. *Bsvr.* 2C **26**
Robert Clo. *Uns.* 3A **6**
Robertson's Av. *Duck* 6G **17**
Robincroft. *Ches* 5B **22**
Robincroft Rd. *Wing* 2H **29**
Rocester Way. *N Wing.* . . . 2H **35**
Rock Cres. *Clay C* 3C **34**
Rockingham Clo. *Ches.* . . . 1G **21**
Rockingham Clo.
Dron W 5A **2**
Rock La. *Sut S.* 6E **25**
Rockley Clo. *Ches* 5A **22**
Rockside Cotts. *Clow.* 5F **19**
Rodge Cft. *Old W.* 5C **6**
Rod Moor Rd. *Dron W* 2A **2**
Rodsley Clo. *Ches* 5F **13**
Rodwood Av. *Blbgh* 1E **11**
Roecar Clo. *Old W.* 6D **6**
Romeley Cres. *Clow* 5H **11**
Romeley La. *Stanf* 6E **11**
Romford Way. *Bar H* 5B **8**
Romney Dri. *Dron* 5C **2**
Rood La. *Clow* 6F **19**
Rose Av. *Cal.* 1A **24**
Rose Av. *Clow* 4H **19**
Rose Cotts. *Ches* 2E **23**
Rose Ct. *Clay C* 4C **34**
Rose Cres. *Mas M.* 4A **10**
Rosedale Av. *Ches.* 4D **22**
Rosedale Vw. *Ches.* 5F **21**
Rosegarth Clo. *Ches* 3E **23**
Rose Hill. *Ches* 1B **22**
Rosehill Ct. *Bsvr* 3E **27**
Rose Hill E. *Ches.* 1C **22**
Rose Hill W. *Ches.* 1B **22**
Rosene Cotts. *Cut* 3C **12**
Rose Wood Clo. *Ches* 2H **13**
Rosling Way. *Ark T* 2D **24**
Rossendale Clo. *Ches.* . . . 4A **22**
Roston Clo. *Dron W* 5B **2**
Rothay Clo. *Dron W.* 6C **2**
Rother Av. *Brim.* 2F **15**
Rother Clo. *Ches.* 4A **22**
Rother Cft. *New T* 6F **31**
Rotherham Rd. *Bsvr.* 4H **27**

Rotherham Rd. *Clow* 4F **19**
Rothervale Rd. *Ches* 4C **22**
. . . . (Derby Rd.)
Rothervale Rd. *Ches* 5C **22**
. . . . (Storforth La.)
Rother Way. *Ches* 4D **14**
Rothey Gro. *Ches* 5D **12**
Rowan Rd. *Mas M.* 5A **10**
Rowsley Cres. *Stav* 2C **16**
Royal Ct. *Ches.* 6C **14**
Royston Clo. *Walt* 5F **21**
Rubens Clo. *Dron* 5D **2**
Rufford Clo. *Ches* 3A **22**
Rushen Mt. *Ches* 6B **22**
Rusk, The. *Blbgh* 2F **11**
Russell Gdns. *Old T.* 2D **34**
Ruston Clo. *Ches* 4F **13**
Ruthyn Av. *Blbgh* 1E **11**
Rutland Av. *Bsvr* 3E **27**
Rutland Rd. *Ches.* 1B **22**
Rutland St. *Old W* 6C **6**
Rutland Ter. *Barl* 5C **4**
Rydal Clo. *Dron W.* 5B **2**
Rydal Cres. *Ches* 2A **14**
Rydal Way. *Clay C* 5D **34**
Rye Ct. *Dane* 5F **35**
Rye Cres. *Dane* 5F **35**
Rye Flatt La. *Ches* 2F **21**
Ryehill Av. *Ches.* 2E **21**
Rykneld Ct. *Clay C* 5E **35**
Rykneld Ri. *Wing.* 3C **30**
Rykneld Sq. Ches 1C **22**
. . . . (off Church Way)

S

Sackville Clo. *Walt* 4F **21**
Saddlers Cft. *N Wing.* 1H **35**
Saddletree Vw. *Mas M.* . . . 4H **9**
St Albans Clo.
Hlmwd 6E **33**
St Andrews Ri. *Ches* 4G **21**
St Anne's Clo. *Stav* 2D **16**
St Augustines. 4C **22**
St Augustines Av.
Ches 4C **22**
St Augustines Cres.
Ches 4C **22**
St Augustines Dri.
Ches 3C **22**
St Augustines Mt.
Ches 4C **22**
St Augustines Ri.
Ches 4C **22**
St Augustines Rd.
Ches 4B **22**
St David's Ri. *Ches* 4H **21**
St Giles Clo. *Ches* 4D **22**
St Helen's Clo. *Ches* 6C **14**
St Helen's St. *Ches* 6C **14**
St James Clo. *Ches* 3E **23**
St James Sq. Ches 1C **22**
. . . . (off Vicar La.)
St Johns Clo. *Walt* 5F **21**
St John's Cres. *Clow* 6G **19**
St John's Mt. *Ches* 2B **14**
St Johns Pl. *Stav.* 1D **16**
St John's Rd. *Ches* 3A **14**
. . . . (in two parts)
St Johns Rd. *Stav* 1C **16**
St John's Rd. *Uns* 1A **6**
St Lawrence Av. *Bsvr.* . . . 3G **27**
St Lawrence Rd.
N Wing 1H **35**
St Leonards Dri.
Ches 3E **23**
St Lukes Ct. *Ches* 2B **14**
St Margaret's Dri.
Ches 1B **22**
St Mark's Rd. *Ches* 1A **22**
St Martin's Clo. *Ches.* 4H **13**

St Mary's & All Saints' Church.
(Crooked Spire) 1D 22
St Mary's Ga. Ches 1D 22
St Mary's Pl. Ches 1D 22
(off St Mary's Ga.)
St Pauls Av. Has 6F 23
St Peters Clo. Duck 6G 17
St Philip's Dri. Has 4D 22
St Quentin Dri. Shef 1A 2
St Quentin Mt. Shef 1A 2
St Quentin Ri. Shef 1A 2
St Quentin Vw. Shef 1A 2
St Thomas St. Ches 2G 21
Salcey Sq. Ches 3H 21
Sales Av. New T 6E 31
Salisbury Av. Ches 3A 14
Salisbury Av. Dron 6E 3
Salisbury Cres. Ches 3B 14
Salisbury Rd. Dron 1F 5
Saltergate. Ches 1B 22
Salvin Cres. Clow 5F 19
Sandhills Rd. Bsvr 3F 27
Sandiway. Ches 4G 21
Sandringham Clo. Cal 6A 16
Sandringham Rd. Cal 6A 16
Sandstone Av. Walt 4F 21
Sanforth St. Ches 4C 14
Scarcliffe. 6H 27
Scarsdale Clo. Dron 6F 3
Scarsdale Cres. Brim 3F 15
Scarsdale Cross. Dron 5F 3
Scarsdale Rd. Ches 2C 14
Scarsdale Rd. Dron 5E 3
Scarsdale St. Bsvr 4C 26
School Board La.
Ches 1A 22
School Clo. Heath 5F 33
Schoolfield Clo. Bsvr 3G 27
School Hill. Cut 3B 12
School La. Ark T 1D 24
School La. Dron 5E 3
School Rd. Ches 3C 14
Scott Clo. Gras 3G 31
Seagrave Dri. Ches 5E 23
Searson Av. Bsvr 3E 27
Searston Av. Hlmwd 6D 32
Sedbergh Cres. Ches 3H 13
Sedgemoor Clo. Ches 6F 13
Selby Clo. Ches 4G 21
Selhurst Rd. Ches 5B 14
Selmer Ct. Brim 2F 15
Selwyn St. Bsvr 4G 27
Setts Way. Wing 2D 30
Severn Cres. N Wing 3H 35
Seymour La. Mas M 1A 18
(in two parts)
Shaftesbury Av. Ches 1H 21
Shafton Clo. Clay C 4G 35
Shafton Wlk. Clay C 4G 35
Shakespeare Clo.
Old T 2D 34
Shakespeare Cres.
Dron 6G 3
Shakespeare St. Gras 3G 31
Shakespeare St.
Hlmwd 5D 32
Shambles, The. Ches 1C 22
(off High St.)
Shamrock Pl. Mas M 4A 10
Shap Clo. Ches 5G 13
Shaws Row. Ches 2H 21
Shaw St. Ches 2C 14
Shaw St. Coal A 2G 3
Shaw St. Hlmwd 5D 32
Sheards Clo. Dron W 4D 2
Sheards Dri. Dron W 5C 2
Sheards Way. Dron W 5D 2
Sheepbridge. 6A 6
Sheepbridge La. Ches 6A 6
Sheepbridge Trad. Est.
Ches 5G 5
Sheepbridge Works.
Ches 6A 6

Sheeplea La. Asvr 6B 28
Sheffield Rd. Ches 2C 14
(in three parts)
Sheffield Rd.
Ches & Uns 5A 6
Sheffield Rd. Clow 5H 19
Sheffield Rd. Dron 3D 2
(in two parts)
Sheffield Rd.
Ren & Blbgh 1B 10
Sheldon Rd. Ches 5F 13
Shelley Dri. Dron 1G 5
Shelley St. Hlmwd 5D 32
Shepley St. Ches 2H 21
Shepleys Yd. Ches 1C 22
Sherbourne Av. Ches 2A 14
Sherwood Pl. Dron W 5B 2
Sherwood Rd. Dron W 5B 2
Sherwood St. Bsvr 4D 26
Sherwood St. Ches 3D 22
Shetland Rd. Dron 6F 3
Shinwell Av. Ink 3B 16
Shire La. Heath 1F 33
Shireoaks Rd. Dron 4G 3
Shirland St. Ches 6C 14
Shirley Clo. Ches 5F 13
Short Clo. Holy 5B 20
Shunters Drift. Blbgh 2F 11
Shuttlewood. 4D 18
Shuttlewood Common.
. . . . 3D 18
Shuttlewood Rd.
Bsvr 4D 18
Sidlaw Clo. Ches 5G 13
Silverdale Clo. Ches 1A 14
Silver Well Dri. Stav 2D 16
Sims Cft. Old W 5E 7
Sitwell Av. Ches 3B 12
Skeldale Dri. Ches 4D 22
Skelwith Clo. Ches 2H 13
Skiddaw Clo. Ches 4H 13
Slack La. Ches 1F 21
Slack La. Heath 3F 33
Slag La. Mar L 2F 7
Slatepit Dale. 1D 28
Slater St. Clay C 5F 35
Slayley Hill. Clow 4G 11
Slayley Vw. Clow 3G 11
Slayley Vw. Rd.
Blbgh 2F 11
Smeckley Wood Clo.
Ches 5G 5
Smeltinghouse La.
Barl 5C 4
Smith Av. Ink 3B 16
Smith Cres. Ches 3F 23
Smithfield Av. Ches 5E 23
Smithson Av. Bsvr 3F 27
Smithy Av. Clay C 4E 35
Smithy Cft. Dron W 4A 2
Smithy Pl. Gras 4H 31
Snape Hill. 4E 3
Snape Hill. Dron 4E 3
Snapehill Clo. Dron 3E 3
Snapehill Cres. Dron 3E 3
Snapehill Dri. Dron 3E 3
Snape Hill La. Dron 4E 3
Snelston Clo. Dron W 5A 2
Snipe Clo. Holy 5B 20
Soaper La. Dron 4E 3
Solway Ri. Dron W 4B 2
Somersall Clo. Ches 3E 21
Somersall Hall Dri.
Ches 4E 21
Somersall La. Ches 4E 21
Somersall Pk. Rd.
Ches 3E 21
Somersall Willows.
Ches 3E 21
Somersby Av. Walt 5F 21
Somerset Dri. Brim 1H 15
Soresby St. Ches 1C 22
South Clo. Uns 2A 6

Southcote Dri. Dron W 5B 2
South Cres. Bsvr 3F 27
South Cres. Duck 5G 17
Southdown Av. Ches 6G 13
South End. 5H 31
Southend. Gras 4H 31
Southfield Av. Has 6F 23
Southfield Dri. Dron 6G 3
Southfield Mt. Dron 6G 3
Southfields. Clow 6G 19
Southgate Cres. Clow 4G 19
Southgate Way.
Bar H 4B 8
S. Lodge Ct. Ches 1F 21
Southmoor Clo. Brim 6H 15
South Pl. Ches 2H 21
(Barker La.)
South Pl. Ches 2C 22
(Beetwell St.)
South St. Ches 2C 22
South St. N. New W 5F 7
South Ter. Cut 3B 12
Southwood Av. Dron 1E 5
Southwood Dri. Clow 6G 19
Sowters Row. Ches 1C 22
(off High St.)
Spa La. Ches 1D 22
(in two parts)
Spancarr. 6C 28
Sparrowbusk Clo.
Blbgh 2F 11
Speedwell Ind. Est.
Stav 1E 17
Speetley Vw. Blbgh 1F 11
Speighthill Cres.
Wing 2A 30
Spencer Av. Mas M 6H 9
Spencer St. Bsvr 4D 26
Spencer St. Ches 6C 14
Spinney, The. Brim 2F 15
Spire Lodge. Ches 5C 14
Spital. 2E 23
Spital Brook Clo.
Ches 3E 23
Spital Gdns. Ches 3E 23
Spital La. Ches 2D 22
Spitewinter. 4C 28
Spittal Grn. Bsvr 4E 27
Springbank. Uns 6H 3
Spring Bank Rd.
Ches 1B 22
Spring Clo. Ren 1A 10
Springfield Av. Ches 1H 21
Springfield Clo. Clow 6F 19
Springfield Cres. Bsvr 1D 26
Springfield Rd.
Barl 5B 4
Springfield Rd.
Hlmwd 6D 32
Spring Ho. Clo. Ash 5D 12
Spring La. Ren 1A 10
Spring Pl. Ches 1C 22
Springvale Clo. Dane 6F 35
Spring Va. Rd. Brim 2F 15
Springvale Rd. Dane 6E 35
Springwell Hill. Mar L 2G 7
Springwell Pk. Dri.
Ink 3C 16
Spring Wood Clo.
Ches 2G 13
Springwood Ct.
New W 4F 7
Springwood St.
Temp N 2B 32
Square, The. Cut 3D 12
Square, The. Dane 5G 35
Stables Ct. Bsvr 3G 27
Stafford Clo. Dron W 4A 2
Stainsby. 6H 33
Stainsby Clo. Hlmwd 6F 33
Stanage Way. Ches 5D 12
Stand Pk. Ind. Est.
Ches 3C 14

Stand Rd. Ches 2B 14
Stanedge Golf Course.
. . . . 2B 28
Stanford Rd. Dron W 5A 2
Stanford Way. Walt 4F 21
Stanfree. 1F 19
Stanley Av. Ink 4B 16
Stanley St. Ches 2E 23
Stanwood Dri. Walt 4F 21
Statham Av. New T 6E 31
Sta. Back La. Ches 1D 22
Station La.
Old W & New W 6D 6
Station La. Ind. Est.
Old W 6D 6
Station New Rd.
Old T 1E 35
Station Rd. Bar H 5B 8
Station Rd. Bsvr 2C 26
Station Rd. Brim 2E 15
Station Rd. Ches 1D 22
Station Rd. Clow 5F 19
Station Rd. Holl 1H 15
Station Rd. N Wing 1G 35
Station Rd. Whit M 1C 14
Station Ter. Brim 2E 15
Staunton Clo. Ches 6C 22
Staveley. 6E 9
Staveley La.
Neth Ha & Stav 1H 7
Staveley La.
Eck & Stav 1E 9
Staveley Rd. Ark T 5E 17
Staveley Rd. New W 5G 7
Staveley Rd. Pool 2F 17
Steele Av. Ink 4B 16
Steel La. Bsvr 2F 27
Steel's La. Pal 6F 27
Steeping Clo. Brim 2G 15
Steep La. Wing 2E 29
Steeplegate. Ches 1C 22
Stephenson Ct. Ches 2F 21
Stephenson Pl. Ches 1C 22
Stephenson Pl.
Clay C 4C 34
Stephenson Rd.
Stav 1E 17
Sterland St. Ches 1A 22
Sterry Clo. Clow 6H 11
Stillman Clo. Has 4E 23
Stockley Vw. Bsvr 4F 27
Stocks La. Duck 1G 25
Stollard St. Clay C 4F 35
Stone Clo. Coal A 3G 3
Stone Edge. 3B 28
Stonegravels. 4C 14
Stonegravels La.
Ches 5C 14
Stoneholes Dri.
Dane 6G 35
Stonelow Ct. Dron 4F 3
(off Stonelow Rd.)
Stonelow Cres. Dron 4G 3
Stonelow Grn. Dron 4F 3
Stonelow Rd. Dron 4F 3
Stone Rd. Coal A 2G 3
Stone Row. Ches 2A 22
Stoneycroft La. Wing 2E 29
Stoops Clo. Ches 4H 13
Stoppard Row. Ches 2G 21
Storforth La.
Ches & Has 5C 22
Storforth La. Ter.
Has 4E 23
Storforth La. Trad. Est.
Has 4D 22
Stormont Gro. Ink 3C 16
Storrs Rd. Ches 2F 21
Stour Clo. Brim 2G 15
Stradbroke Ri. Ches 4G 21
Stretton Rd. Bsvr 2E 27
Stretton Rd. Clay C 6E 35

Stride, The. *Ches* 5B **22**
Stuart Clo. *Ches*. 4E **15**
Stubbing Rd. *Ches*. 5B **22**
Stubley Clo. *Dron W* 3C **2**
Stubley Cft. *Dron W*. 4B **2**
Stubley Dri. *Dron W* 4C **2**
Stubley Hollow. *Dron*. . . . 4C **2**
Stubley La. *Dron* 4B **2**
Stubley Pl. *Dron* 4C **2**
Studios, The. 1A **22**
(off School Board La.)
Sub-Station La.
. . . . *Ches* 2C **14**
(off Queen St. N.)
Sudbury Clo. *Ches* 5F **13**
Sudhall Clo. *Ches* 2H **13**
Sudhall Ct. *Ches* 2H **13**
Summerfield Cres.
. . . . *Brim* 2F **15**
Summerfield Rd.
. . . . *Ches* 3B **22**
Summerfield Rd. *Dron*. . . . 3F **3**
Summerley Wlk.
. . . . *Ches* 5H **13**
Summerskill Grn. *Ink*. . . . 3C **16**
Summerwood La.
. . . . *Dron* 3D **2**
Summerwood Pl. *Dron* . . . 4D **2**
Sunningdale Clo.
. . . . *Ches* 4A **22**
Sunningdale Pk. Cvn. Pk.
. . . . *New T* 5E **31**
Sunningdale Ri. *Ches* . . . 4G **21**
Sunny Brook Clo.
. . . . *Clow* 6F **19**
Sunny Springs. *Ches*. . . . 6C **14**
Sutton Cres. *Ink*. 3C **16**
Sutton Hall Rd. *Bsvr* 4C **26**
Sutton La. *Sut S* 2D **24**
Sutton Scarsdale. 6G **25**
Sutton Scarsdale Hall.
. . . . 6G **25**
Sutton Spring Wood.
. . . . 6B **24**
Sutton Vw. *Bsvr*. 4F **27**
Swaddale Av. *Ches* 4D **14**
Swaddale Clo. *Ches*. 4D **14**
Swalebank Clo. *Ches*. . . . 4D **22**
Swanbourne Clo. *Ches*. . . 4E **23**
Swanwick St. *Old W* 6C **6**
Swathwick. 2A **30**
Swathwick Clo. *Wing*. . . . 2A **30**
Swathwick La. *Wing* 2D **28**
Swinger La. *Asvr*. 6B **28**
Swinscoe Way. *Ches* 5E **13**
Swithland Clo. *Ches* 5E **23**
Sycamore Av. *Ches* 3A **22**
Sycamore Av. *Dron* 3E **3**
Sycamore Clo. *Bsvr*. 2G **27**
Sycamore Dri. *Cal* 1G **23**
Sycamore La. *Blbgh*. 2F **11**
Sycamore La. *Holl* 1A **16**
Sycamore Rd. *Holl* 1H **15**
Sydney St. *Ches* 1A **22**
Sylvan Clo. *Ches* 3D **22**
Sylvan Dri. *Old T* 2C **34**
Sylvia Rd. *Uns*. 2H **5**

T

Taddington Rd. *Ches* 5F **13**
Talbot Cres. *Has*. 5F **23**
Talbot St. *Has*. 5F **23**
Tallys End. *Blbgh* 2E **11**
Tansley Dri. *Ches* 5E **13**
Tansley Rd. *N Wing*. 3H **35**
Tansley Way. *Ink* 4C **16**
Tap La. *Ches* 1A **22**
Tapton.. . . . . 4E **15**
Tapton Grange. *Brim* 5G **15**
Tapton Gro. *Brim*. 5G **15**

Tapton La. *Ches*. 1D **22**
Tapton Lock Hill.
. . . . *Ches*. 4D **14**
Tapton Lock Vis. Cen.
. . . . 4D **14**
**Tapton Pk. Municipal Golf
Course.** 6E **15**
Tapton Ter. *Ches*. 6D **14**
Tapton Va. *Ches* 5E **15**
Tapton Vw. Rd. *Ches* 5B **14**
Tapton Way. *Cal*. 1H **23**
Tay Clo. *Dron W* 4B **2**
Taylor Cres. *Ches* 3F **23**
Telford Cres. *Ches* 6F **9**
Temple Normanton. 3B **32**
Temple Normanton Bus. Pk.
. . . . *Cor* 2A **32**
Temple Normanton By-Pass.
. . . . *Temp N* 2B **32**
Tennyson Av. *Ches*. 1B **22**
Tennyson St. *Hlmwd* 5D **32**
Tennyson Way. *Gras* 3G **31**
Thanet St. *Clay C* 5E **35**
Theatre La. *Ches* 1D **22**
Theatre Yd. Ches 1C **22**
(off Low Pavement)
Thirlmere Rd. *Dron* 4E **3**
Thirlmere Rd. *Ches*. 3G **13**
Thirteen Row. *Pal*. 6E **27**
Thompson Clo. *Ches* 2C **14**
Thompson St. *Ches* 2C **14**
. . . . . . *(Brimington Rd.)*
Thompson St. *Ches* 3C **14**
. . . . *(King St. N.)*
Thoresby Av. *Clow*. 5H **19**
Thoresby Pl. *Ink* 4C **16**
Thornbridge Cres.
. . . . *Ches*. 6B **22**
Thorndene Clo. *Ches*. . . . 4C **14**
Thorndon Way. *Ches* 4G **21**
Thorne Clo. *Ash*. 6D **12**
Thornfield Av. *Ches* 3F **21**
Thornfield Ct. *Ches* 5C **14**
Thornton Pl. *Dron W* 5A **2**
Thorntree Ct. *Ches*. 5B **22**
Thorpe Av. *Coal A* 2G **3**
Thorpe Clo. *Ches* 2B **14**
Thorpleigh Rd.
. . . . *Mas M* 6H **9**
Tibshelf Rd. *Hlmwd*. 6D **32**
Tideswell Clo. *Stav*. 2B **16**
Tissington Clo. *Ches* 5F **13**
Tollbridge Rd. *Mas M* . . . 6H **9**
Tom La. *Duck*. 5E **17**
Tontine Rd. *Ches* 2C **22**
Top Pingle Clo. *Brim* 3G **15**
Top Rd. *Cal* 2H **23**
Top Rd. *Wing*. 5H **29**
Torrani Way. *N Wing* 1H **35**
Totley Mt. *Brim*. 2F **15**
Tourist Info. Cen. 1C **22**
. . . . *(Chesterfield)*
Tower Bus. Cen. *Clay C* . . 4E **35**
Tower Cres. *Bsvr*. 4F **27**
Town End. *Bsvr* 3E **27**
Traffic Ter. *Bar H* 4B **8**
Traffic Ter. *Has*. 5D **22**
Tramere Av. *Clay C*. 5F **35**
Tree Neuk Clo. *Ches*. 1F **21**
Trelawney Rd. *Clay C* 5F **35**
Trent Gro. *Dron* 3F **3**
Trevose Clo. *Ches* 5G **21**
Trinity Clo. *Ches*. 6B **14**
Troon Clo. *Ches*. 4G **21**
Troughbrook Hill.
. . . . . . *Stav* 2C **16**
Troughbrook Rd. *Holl* 1B **16**
Tudor St. *Stav*. 6F **9**
Tunstall Grn. *Ches*. 3H **21**
Tunstall Way. *Ches* 3H **21**
Tupton. 6F **31**
Tupton Moor Clo.
. . . . *Old T* 5F **31**

Tupton Way. *Hlmwd* 5D **32**
Turnberry Clo. *Ches*. 4G **21**
Turnbull Clo. *Ches* 3B **22**
Turner Clo. *Dron* 5D **2**
Turner Dri. *Ink* 2B **16**
Turnoaks Bus. Pk.
. . . . *Ches*. 5D **22**
Turnoaks La. *Ches*. 5C **22**
. . . . . . *(in three parts)*
Twentywell Dri. *Shef* 1A **2**
Twentywell La. *Shef*. 1A **2**
Tylney Rd. *Ches* 4F **21**

U

Ullswater Clo. *Dron W* . . . 4C **2**
Ullswater Dri. *Dron W* . . . 5C **2**
Ullswater Pk. *Dron W* . . . 4C **2**
Ullswater Pl. *Dron W* 4C **2**
Ulverston Rd. *Ches* 3H **13**
Underhill Rd. *Blbgh*. 2F **11**
Union Wlk. *Ches* 1C **22**
Unstone. 1A **6**
Unstone-Dronfield By-Pass.
. . . . *Dron* 5D **2**
Unstone Green. 3A **6**
Unstone Hill. *Uns* 6H **3**
Unstone Rd. *Ches* 3B **6**
Upland Ri. *Ches* 3H **21**
Upper Cft. *Dane* 5F **35**
Upper Cft. *New T* 6F **31**
Up. Croft Clo. *Brim* 3G **15**
Up. King St. *Brim* 1H **15**
Up. Lum Clo. *Ches*. 2F **23**
Up. Mantle Clo.
. . . . *Clay C* 4E **35**
Up. Mill Cotts. *Alt* 3A **34**
Up. Moor St. *Ches* 2F **21**
Upper Newbold. 2E **13**
Up. Newbold Clo.
. . . . *Ches* 3F **13**
Up. School La. *Dron*. 6F **3**
Upwood Clo. *Ches* 5E **13**

V

Vale Clo. *Bsvr*. 3E **27**
Vale Clo. *Dron* 5F **3**
Valley Cres. *Ches*. 2E **23**
Valley Ri. *Barl* 5B **4**
Valley Rd. *Barl* 4B **4**
Valley Rd. *Bsvr*. 4E **27**
Valley Rd. *Ches* 2E **23**
Valley Rd. *Clay C* 4C **34**
Valley Rd. *Mas M*. 4A **10**
Valley Vw. *Bsvr* 5F **27**
Valley Vw. Clo. *Has* 5G **23**
Vanguard Trad. Est.
. . . . *Ches* 5D **22**
Venture Way. *Ches*. 1B **14**
Vernon Ri. *Gras*. 4H **31**
Vernon Rd. *Ches* 1H **21**
Vicarage Clo. *Heath*. 4H **33**
Vicarage Gdns.
. . . . *Clay C* 6E **35**
Vicar La. *Ches* 1C **22**
Victoria Av. *Stav*. 5F **9**
Victoria Gro. *Brim* 5H **15**
Victoria Pk. Rd. *Brim*. . . . 5H **15**
Victoria St. *Bsvr*. 4F **27**
Victoria St. *Brim* 5H **15**
Victoria St. *Ches* 6C **14**
Victoria St. *Clay C* 5E **35**
Victoria St. *Dron* 4D **2**
Victoria St. N. *Old W* 6B **6**
Victoria St. W. *Ches*. 2G **21**
Victoria Wlk. *New T* 5E **31**
Villas Rd. *Bsvr*. 2C **26**
Vincent Cres. *Ches*. 2F **21**

Vincent La. *Ches* 2F **21**
Vivian St. *Shut*. 4D **18**

W

Wain Av. *Ches* 1D **22**
Walgrove Av. *Ches*. 3A **22**
Walgrove Rd. *Ches* 3H **21**
Wallsend Cotts. *Ches*. . . . 5A **14**
Waltham Cft. *Ches* 5E **23**
Walton. 4F **21**
Walton Bk. La. *Walt*. 5C **20**
Walton Clo. *Ches* 4F **21**
Walton Clo. *Dron W* 4A **2**
Walton Cres. *Ches* 3A **22**
Walton Dri. *Ches* 3A **22**
Walton Dri. *Ches* 3A **22**
Waltonfields Rd.
. . . . *Ches*. 2H **21**
WALTON HOSPITAL. 5A **22**
Walton Rd. *Ches* 2H **21**
Walton Wlk. *Ches* 2A **22**
Walton Way. *Wing* 2A **30**
Walton Works. *Ches* 2H **21**
Wardgate Way. *Ches* 5E **13**
Ward La. *Blbgh* 1E **11**
Wardlow Clo. *Ches* 4B **22**
Ward St. *New T* 6F **31**
Ward's Yd. Ches 2C **22**
. . . . . . *(off Beetwell St.)*
Warner St. *Ches* 3D **22**
Warren Ri. *Dron* 3G **3**
Warwick St. *Ches* 5D **22**
Warwick St. Ind. Est.
. . . . *Ches* 5D **22**
Wash Ho. La. *Ches* 2G **21**
Watercress La. *Dane* 6F **35**
Wateringbury Gro.
. . . . . . *Stav* 6F **9**
Water La. *Ches* 4C **26**
Waterloo St. *Clay C* 4E **35**
Water Mdw. La. *Ches* 3F **13**
Watson La. *Wing* 3G **29**
Wayford St. *Has* 3D **22**
Wayside. *Brim*. 2F **15**
Wayside Clo. *N Wing*. . . . 1H **35**
Wayside Ct. *Brim* 2F **15**
Way, The. *Ches* 4F **21**
Webster Ct. *Ches*. 5A **14**
. . . . . . *(off Newbold Bk. La.)*
Webster Cft. *Old W* 6D **6**
Welbeck Clo. *Dron W* . . . 4A **2**
Welbeck Clo. *Ink* 4D **16**
Welbeck Ct. *Clow*. 6G **19**
Welbeck Dri. *Wing* 2A **30**
Welbeck Rd. *Bsvr*. 3F **27**
Welbeck Vs. *Bsvr* 2F **27**
Welfare Av. *Ches* 1H **21**
Wellbeck Ct. Stav. 6E **9**
. . . . . . *(off Devonshire St.)*
Wellington St. *New W* . . . 4F **7**
Wellspring Clo.
. . . . *Blbgh*. 2F **11**
Well Spring Clo.
. . . . *Blbgh* 3G **15**
Wellspring Clo. *Wing*. . . . 2D **30**
Wells St. *Bsvr* 4G **27**
Welshpool Pl. *Ches* 1H **21**
Welshpool Yd. *Ches* 2H **21**
Welwyn Clo. *Ches*. 1H **21**
Wenlock Clo. *Ches*. 6H **13**
Wenlock Cres. *Ches* 6G **13**
Wenlock Dri. *Gras* 3H **31**
Wenlock Wlk. *Gras* 3H **31**
Wensley Rd. *N Wing* 3H **35**
Wensley Way. *Stav* 2C **16**
Wentworth Av. *Ches* 4A **22**
Wentworth Rd.
. . . . *Dron W* 5A **2**
Wessington Dri. *Stav*. . . . 2C **16**

Westbank Clo. *Coal A.* 2F **3**
Westbank Ct. *Coal A* 2G **3**
West Bars. *Ches* 1B **22**
Westbourne Gro. *Ches.* . . . 1F **21**
Westbridge Rd. *Blbgh* 1E **11**
Westbrook Clo. *Ches.* 2D **20**
Westbrook Dri. *Ches.* 2D **20**
West Cres. *Duck* 5G **17**
West Cft. Ct. *Ink* 5B **16**
West Cft. Dri. *Ink* 5B **16**
West End. *Blbgh* 1E **11**
W. End Bungalows.
  Blbgh *1E 11*
      (off West End)
Westfield Av. *Ches* 3F **21**
Westfield Bank. *Blbgh* 1E **11**
Westfield Clo. *Ches* 2F **21**
Westfield Gdns. *Ches.* 2F **21**
Westfield La. *Blbgh* 1D **10**
Westfield La. *Mid H.* 1H **7**
Westfield Rd. *Dron* 6G **3**
West Handley. 1F **7**
Westhill La. *Gras* 3G **31**
Westlands. *Bar H.* 5B **8**
West Lea. *Ches* 2F **21**
W. Lea Cotts. *Clow* 4H **11**
Westlea Vw. *Clow* 4H **11**
Westleigh Ct. *Ches.* 5A **14**
Westmoor Rd. *Brim.* 6H **15**
Weston Clo. *Ches.* 4E **13**
West St. *Ches* 6B **14**
West St. *Clay C* 4C **34**
West St. *Clow* 4H **19**
West St. *Dron* 4D **2**
West Vw. *Blbgh* 1E **11**
West Vw. *Bsvr* 4F **27**
West Vw. *Stav.* 1D **16**
W. View Rd. *Ches* 4A **14**
Westwick La. *Holy* 2B **20**
Westwood Av. *Stav* 2C **16**
Westwood Clo. *Ink.* 5C **16**
Westwood Dri. *Ink.* 5C **16**
Westwood Dri. Gdns.
  Ink 5B **16**
Westwood La. *Brim.* 6H **15**
Westwood Rd. *Cal.* 6A **16**
Wetlands La. *Ches.* 6G **15**
Whaley Rd. *Bsvr* 1H **27**
Wharf La. *Ches* 6C **14**
Wharf La. *Stav.* 5F **9**
Wharton Dri. *Ches.* 1D **22**
Wheatbridge Retail Pk.
  Ches 2B **22**
Wheatbridge Rd. *Ches.* . . . 1A **22**
Wheatcroft Clo. *Dane.* 6F **35**
Wheatcroft Clo. *Wing* 2C **30**
Wheatfield Way. *Ash* 5D **12**

Wheathill Clo. *Ash* 6D **12**
Wheathill Clo. *Brim* 6H **15**
Wheathill La. *Ches.* 6F **15**
Wheatlands Rd. *Wing* 2A **30**
Wheeldon Cres. *Brim.* 2F **15**
Whinacre Wlk. *Shef.* 1E **3**
Whitebank Clo. *Ches.* 3D **22**
Whitecotes Clo. *Ches.* 4A **22**
Whitecotes La. *Ches.* 4A **22**
Whitecotes Pk. *Ches.* 4B **22**
White Edge Clo. *Ches.* . . . 5H **13**
Whitehead St. *Stav.* 6F **9**
Whitehouses. *Ches.* 3D **22**
White Leas. *Ches.* 6F **13**
White Leas Av.
  N Wing . . . . 6A **32** & 1H **35**
Whites Cft. Vw. Blbgh *2F 11*
     (off Bracken La.)
White Thorns Clo. *Shef* . . . 1F **3**
White Thorns Dri. *Shef* . . . 1F **3**
White Thorns Vw. *Shef* . . . 1F **3**
Whitmore Av. *Gras* 4G **31**
Whittington Hill.
  Old W. 1C **14**
Whittington La. *Uns.* 2A **6**
Whittington Moor. 2C **14**
Whittington Rd. *Bar H.* 4G **7**
Whittington Way.
  Whit M 1C **14**
Whitting Valley Rd.
  Old W. 1C **14**
Whitton Pl. *Duck.* 4G **17**
Whitworth Rd. *Ches* 4B **14**
Wholey Pl. *Clay C* 5E **35**
Wickens Pl. *Mas M* 4H **9**
Wigley Rd. *Ink.* 4C **16**
Wikeley Way. *Brim.* 2F **15**
Wilday Green. 6A **4**
Wildaygreen La. *Barl* 6A **4**
Wilkin Hill. *Barl* 1C **12**
Williamthorpe. 6D **32**
Williamthorpe Clo.
  N Wing 1H **35**
Williamthorpe Ponds.
  (Nature Reserve) . . . 4D **32**
Williamthorpe Rd.
  N Wing . . . 1H **35** & 6A **32**
Willow Ct. *Cal* 1A **24**
Willow Dri. *Mas M.* 4A **10**

Willow Gth. Rd. *Ches* . . . 2G **13**
Willow Tree Dri. *Clow* . . . 6G **19**
Wilson Av. *Clow.* 4G **19**
Wilson Clo. *Dane* 6F **35**
Wilson La. *Heath.* 4H **33**
Wilson Rd. *Coal A* 2G **3**
Wilson St. *Dron* 6F **3**
Wimborne Cres. *Ches.* . . . 3A **14**
Winchester Clo.
  N Wing 2H **35**
Winchester Rd. *Ches.* . . . 3A **14**
Windermere Av.
  Dron W. 5C **2**
Windermere Rd.
  Ches 3G **13**
Windermere Rd.
  Clay C 5D **34**
Winders Corner.
  Blbgh. 3F **11**
Windmill Clo. *Bsvr.* 1E **27**
Windmill La. *App.* 3C **6**
Windsor Clo. *Ches.* 3G **21**
Windsor Dri. *Dron W.* 5A **2**
Windsor Dri. *Wing.* 3A **30**
Windsor Wlk. *Has* 3E **23**
Windy Fields Rd.
  Holy 5B **20**
Wingerworth. *Ches* 2C **30**
Wingerworth Cotts.
  Gras 3G **31**
Wingerworth Hall.
  Wing. 3C **30**
Wingerworth Hall Est.
  Wing *3C 30*
     (off Lodge Dri.)
Wingerworth St. *Gras* . . . 3G **31**
Wingerworth Way.
  Ches 6B **22**
Wingfield Clo. *Dron W.* . . . 5A **2**
Wingfield Rd. *New T* 6F **31**
Winnat Pl. *Ink* 3C **16**
Winnats Clo. *Ches.* 5G **13**
Winsick. 6G **23**
Winster Clo. *Old T.* 3C **34**
Winster Ct. *Ches* 6C **14**
Winster Rd. *Stav.* 2C **16**
Wisbech Clo. *Ches.* 4A **22**
Wiston Way *Ches.* 5E **23**
Witham Clo. *Ches.* 4E **15**
Witham Ct. *Ches.* 1G **21**
Wolfcote Clo. *Dane.* 6F **35**
Wolfe Clo. *Ches.* 3H **21**
Woodbridge Ri. *Ches.* 4F **21**
Wood Clo. *Wing* 2H **29**
Woodford Way. *Bar H* 4B **8**
Woodhead. 6A **34**
Woodhead La. *Clay C.* 6A **34**

Woodhouse La. *Bsvr.* 6C **18**
Woodhouse La.
  Mas M 3A **10**
Woodhouse Rd. *Bsvr.* 2D **26**
Woodland Gro. *Blbgh.* 2E **11**
Woodland Gro. *Clow* 5H **19**
Woodland Gro. *Old T.* 1D **34**
Woodland Rd. *Ches.* 4B **6**
Woodlands. *Brim* 3F **15**
Woodland Wlk. *Ches.* 5D **12**
Woodland Way. *Old T* . . . 3D **34**
Woodleigh Clo. *Ches.* 5D **12**
Woodmere Dri. *Old W* 4E **7**
Woodnook. 5D **12**
Woodnook Clo. *Ash.* 6D **12**
Woodnook La. *Cut.* 5D **12**
Woodnook Way. *Ash.* 6D **12**
Woodside Clo. *Ches.* 6F **13**
Woodside Pl. *Clay C* 4D **34**
Woodstock Dri. *Has.* 4E **23**
Woodstock Ri. *Has* 4E **23**
Wood St. *Hlmwd* 5E **33**
Woodthorpe. 6A **10**
Woodthorpe Av.
  Clay C 4C **34**
Woodthorpe Clo.
  Shut 4D **18**
Woodthorpe Rd.
  Mas M 6A **10**
Woodthorpe Rd. *Shut* . . . 1C **18**
Woodvale Clo. *Ches.* 4E **21**
Woodview Clo. *Wing* 3B **30**
Woolley Clo. *Old T.* 1D **34**
Wordsworth Pl. *Dron.* 1G **5**
Wordsworth Rd.
  Ches 2B **14**
Works La. *Cal* 2B **24**
Worksop Rd. *Blbgh* 6G **9**
Works Rd. *Holl* 5B **8**
Wreakes La. *Dron* 3D **2**
Wren Pk. Clo. *Ches.* 5B **22**
Wrenpark Rd. *Wing.* 2H **29**
Wyedale Ct. *Ches.* 3A **14**
Wynd, The. *Ren.* 1H **9**
Wythburn Rd. *Ches.* 3G **13**

Y

Yarncliff Clo. *Ches.* 5H **13**
Yeldersley Clo. *Ches.* 5F **13**
Yew Tree Dri. *Ches* 4D **20**
Yew Tree Dri. *Old T.* 2D **34**
York Pl. *N Wing* 6B **32**
York St. *Ches.* 5E **23**